ALL
THINGS
THROUGH
CHRIST

VALUES AT WORK:
ONE PASTOR'S JOURNEY

GARY J. OLSON

ENDORSEMENTS

"Pastor Gary Olson presents a candid, nostalgic reflection on God's presence and provision throughout his life and ministry and in so doing invites and encourages readers to reflect on God's activity in their lives and continue to trust in the God fully revealed in Jesus Christ."

—Robert Ericson, Visitation and Teaching Pastor, Nazareth Lutheran Church, Cedar Falls, Iowa

"Pastor Gary Olson has provided an honest and personal account of not only his personal journey to sustain his joy in daily ministry, but also to reconnect with 'quiet boldness in day-to-day ministry.' Pastor Olson, through each vignette, gives compelling and vivid illustrations that can provide personal insight to wisdom and allow us to renew our Christian belief that Christ's promises are real, a belief that our world desperately needs to embrace."

—Sandra Gardner, DNP, MS, RN, CPAN

"A pastor takes the gifts that God gives to all believers: faith and people of faith. Then that pastor shares those gifts in wonder and hope to the world around us. Academics call it being a resident theologian. Church folks recognize it as pastoral care. This book is one pastor's story of his unique journey to blessing."

—Darrel Gerrietts, retired pastor from Assistant to the Bishop, Northeast Iowa Synod

"Inspiring, heartwarming, down-to-earth sharing of God's intervention, guidance and provision over 50 years fulfilling God's Call. A true testimony of 'I can do all things through Christ.'"

—Byron and Sondra Simar, YWAM Ministries,
Waterloo, Iowa

"What a joy to see how God has been present and at work from the very beginning in the life of one man! Reading Pastor Olson's memoirs has reminded me of how his passion and steadfastness in serving Jesus Christ has made a difference in so many lives—our family as well. All who have known Pastor Olson—and even those who haven't—will be blessed by reading this book, for it inspires us to rekindle our passion for serving our Lord and Savior, Jesus Christ!"

—Janet Mennen, Bethel Lutheran Church,
Parkersburg, Iowa

Table of Contents

FOREWORD

Gary and Ella Olson have ministered to us throughout our years in Cedar Falls, Iowa, and beyond. Ben was senior pastor at Nazareth Lutheran Church while I worked as a nurse educator at NewAldaya. Communicating love to residents, staff and family members came so naturally to them—whether it was by decorating the chapel area beautifully according to each season, welcoming people warmly and calling each by name, telling stories that even those with Alzheimer's could relate to, playing the violin or guitar and singing old hymns or praying the Lord's Prayer—each touching the most vulnerable as well as the most educated.

They touched our hearts with love in a personal way as they reached out to us as daughter/son-in-law of two special residents, my parents, Ted and Tavia Maakestad. They bridged the gap as Ben and I moved to Berlin, Germany, to do ministry. The congregation at NewAldaya was a support to this ELCA ministry, prayerfully and financially. My parents were thrilled. During my parents' final days, Gary and Ella gave personalized, spiritual care to all of us reminding us of the truths of God's Word.

Gary has a treasure trove of stories of faith from his vast experience in ministry that touched us and many others. I am sure that as you read this book you too will be blessed as you are reminded of the faithfulness of God as He has worked through two, dedicated servants—Gary and Ella.

Margit and Ben Coltvet
International Emissaries

INTRODUCTION

Stories and experiences related in this book intend to remind and reassure readers of the promises and presence of Jesus, the Christ, in all circumstances for the believing Christian. We live at a time in history when we keep hearing that the number of people who say they do not need the church is growing. The life-changing Word of God has not changed, but our increasingly secularized culture has changed the mindset of many people. Jesus the Christ continues "the same yesterday, today and forever" (Hebrews 13:8) precious friend for all who love and trust him. We are too often like a cut flower—forgetting the roots out of which have grown some of the most compassionate enterprises of our society. Experience becomes the best teacher to help the believing Christian know that the Lord's promises are as trustworthy today as they have always been. His promises are real and true for life. The words of Jesus in His Gospel of John 7:17 state, "If anyone chooses to do God's will, he will find out whether my teaching comes from God or whether I speak on my own."

Using a thought thread from the book *Open Mind O-pen Heart* (Thomas Keating, 1992), one ideal of the spiritual journey is to be contemplative: listening to the word, having an active will, and resting in the divine presence of his words.

Boldness has been a theme in the area of the church in which I'm privileged to serve; along with the larger church theme, "God's Work in Our Hands." It is the hope and prayer of this writer that these stories, illustrations and references aid in appreciation of some quiet boldness in day-to-day parish ministry, and God's work in our hands. Holy Spirit guided friendship that encourages bold leadership, resonates as a powerful force in the lives of Christians. One story from a friend in Christ can jumpstart a new initiative in ministry. Recently, I attended a chaplain's conference in St. Louis, Missouri. In conversation with a Vietnam veteran suffering post-traumatic stress syndrome and now cancer, I grew through his passion for ministry to veterans and persons in jail.

Boldness in ministry (whether priesthood of all believers, or ordained ministry), I believe, does not have to mean facing a firing squad or facing circumstances that could mean dying as a martyr. Boldness can also mean working to do the right thing even around people who may not appreciate a particular action. For example, when I walk into a dining room as chaplain where I serve in Cedar Falls, Iowa, in a nursing home setting, and I interrupt residents enjoying their meal, a few may not appreciate such an interruption for a table prayer, and/or brief devotion; although most probably do. Nevertheless, it is the chaplain's duty to lead that devotion and prayer. In such circumstances, I seem to hear the Spirit say that faithfulness before even those who may not appreciate one's presence takes a certain amount of boldness. Memories of Joshua's and Moses' stories spur me into increased faithfulness in ministry.

* * * * *

Living and experiencing signs and wonders of spiritual promise and presence helps sustain joy in daily ministry. A beautifully feathered robin became an important teacher to me—one of several motivations to write this book. That bird as teacher/encourager has continued through the years and is a kind of anchor story for this writing. That more complete scenario will appear in a later chapter; and it reminds me of a St. Francis story, "Sermon to the Birds." Here are a few of the words of St. Francis' "Sermon to the Birds" published in a book on his writings and prayers by Wyatt North. "My little sisters, the birds, much bounden are ye unto God, your Creator, and always in every place ought ye to praise Him, for he hath given you liberty to fly about everywhere, and has given you double and triple raiment; ..., my little sisters, beware of the sin of ingratitude, and study always to give praises unto God."

In our upstairs bedroom as children growing up on a farm in west central Wisconsin, mother obviously had been contemplating her children's faith development. Consequently, she hung a plaque on my bedroom wall which read, "I can do all things through him who gives me strength" (Philippians 4:13). Those words of scripture have often been my refuge and strength. Repeating them brings me peace.

Those words appear as the title of this book *All Things Through Christ*. Christ gives strength in many ways: He is co-creator of awesome bodies, He is giver of the Holy Spirit, He has built his church in which we grow in strength by fellowship with one another. Numerous are the ways he continues to give us strength. His Word in the Bible is an endless supply of energy and inspiration.

* * * * *

Quiet Power & Steeple Memories

Skylines of the cities have changed with the passing of many years. Recently, while in New York for a concert at the Lincoln Center, in which two of our grandchildren were playing their instruments, (grandson on cello; granddaughter on trumpet), we walked along a street near Central Park. That walk pays tribute to the marvels of the architecture of recent decades. Once the tallest outstanding images on the skyline of cities were church steeples. Today that skyline is more apt to be dominated by tall buildings, as on Central Avenue in New York: banks, insurance company buildings and other business enterprises.

Spiritual presence may not be as obvious today in many places as in years past; however, for persons with an awareness of the promises of Scripture, the presence and counsel of the Holy Spirit exists everywhere his children wait upon Him for teaching and guidance. In the Gospel, according to St. John, we find these words of Jesus as he's speaking of the Holy Spirit, "I will not leave you orphaned: I am coming to you" (John 14:18). "Anyone who resolves to do the will of God will know whether the teaching is from God or whether I am speaking on my own" (John 7:17). "If you continue in my word, you really are my disciples; and you will know the truth and the truth will make you free" (John 8:31-32).

A hill on our farm in Wisconsin sloped gently south toward the country church about a mile away. There across a river stands that church building with a steeple on the bell tower. That winding river has been named the Beef River. It flows east and west about one-eighth mile away from the country church; therefore, the church site was named South Beef River Lutheran Church.

As children, we were taught the Christian faith in Sunday School, which met in the basement of that country church building; an elegant brick structure. Exuberant, joyful, loving and lovely Christian women leading opening Sunday School devotions remains a vivid and pleasant memory. For years, my mother played the organ and Dad sang in the choir. The choir gathered around the organ at the west end of the wrap-around balcony. Such an elegant interior remains today bordered by lovely stained glass windows. When it was time for worship, our family always sat on the left (lectern side), second pew behind the beautiful wood railing. From that usual place, we could see friends, extended family members and neighbors find their preferred seating places on the first floor.

Habits of worship were formed observing and listening from that balcony view. One man, who happened to be my uncle, sang so loudly that he practically led the congregation in singing. He became, due to my high regard for him, my image of how to sing in church—at the top of one's voice. Ed was a dairy farmer and faithful participant in those worship experiences.

Our children some years later, would hear me as I sat beside them at worship, Dad to the right, family to the left. By this time, we were seated downstairs as visitors. Soon, it occurred to me that during the singing part of worship they were glancing at one another as if thinking how to mellow the voice of this loud worshipper beside them. Soon it occurred to me that they were looking at me somewhat strangely. Their body language had its intended affect. It became apparent to me that their view on congregational singing was to blend with the voices around you, rather than singing like a lone ranger on a horse. That's just one of the many times our children have nurtured me. Since then I've tried to blend with others in congregational singing.

Today that lovely old church building continues to be a Christian nurture center. Through the years, that steeple has become an even greater testimony made possible by the construction of Highway 90 extending from Chicago to the Twin Cities and beyond. One portion of that highway stretches within one-fourth mile of that country church. (One can imagine that from heaven those construction workers can now visualize that their steeple building handiwork is seen by people from around the world who travel that highway.) At the time of building that country church with bell tower and steeple, those builders were probably not imagining an international audience glancing that way as they travelled between those major cities. One more example of the many ways our Heavenly Father blesses faithfulness beyond our ability to ask or think. That realization causes me to hope and pray, that perhaps this book message may have a larger than expected audience too.

Little did I realize, as a child, the influence that piece of architecture would have upon my future. The steeple I saw in the distance as a child and teenager, continues to bless me in many wonderful ways. While walking down the hill on our farm, the hill to the east of the barn, I could see the church steeple above the trees. Even now, seventy-five plus years later, I can relive those moments of seeing the steeple above the tree tops. It represents a nurture center, which helped launch me into life; by my baptism, confirmation, family league, regular worship with family, neighbors and friends, and eventually marriage at that altar at age twenty-eight. That steeple is among the mysteries I ponder while asking "How did I become who I am today?" I am the first male on either my immediate maternal or paternal side of the family tree to receive a college degree; and (so far as I know) the only person of our family for at least several generations past to become a pastor.

The answer to that question for me, as perhaps for many others, involves hundreds, perhaps thousands of influences from the prayers of parents, to conversations with a multitude of people, a few adversities, readings, teachers, professors, and so much more.

CHAPTER ONE
Precious Memories, How They Linger

"If you abide in me, and my words abide in you, ask whatever you wish, and it will be done for you... I have said these things to you so that my joy may be in you, and that your joy may be complete" (John 15:7a,11).

Recently at a family reunion on the home farm in Wisconsin, loving voices echoed through the trees on that summer day in 2013 when grandchildren of my parents had turned the front porch of our childhood country home, one mile from that elegant church building across the river, into a stage for a Christian dance performance put on by the newly formed Karar Dance Academy.

Perfect weather prevailed that day. We had finished our annual family reunion meal always served on tables set up in the four-stall garage within twenty feet of that two-story white wood frame house. As a child, I, as did my siblings, slept in those upstairs bedrooms. A grove of trees and berry bushes wrap around that piece of land to the north and to the east. Fresh water springs continue to flow on that property, one about one hundred yards to the east and another about fifty yards up the pathway through the grove of trees to the west. In that rustic setting, sun shining, birds singing, the family was gathered on the front lawn beneath large trees. The Karar Dance Academy staged their performance from the front porch. Elegantly dressed in ruffled finery, skirts to the floor, these young ladies danced and sang their Christian Karar Academy message.

The originator of the Karar Academy is Holly, the daughter of my youngest brother. They have by the time of this writing travelled hundreds of miles to put on their performances proclaiming the Gospel through dance, music and personal testimonies. Holly's daughter, Elizabeth, has a vision to take this manner of Christian witness to places in Africa.

While watching and listening to that performance on the front porch on that cloudless, sunny, beautiful summer day, I looked over my shoulder to the southeast. There I saw that church building with the elegant steeple and thought of our parents in Heaven. I imagined them rejoicing over what was happening on the front porch of that farm, the farmstead on which they raised their children. That moment became another sign of divine blessing and Spiritual presence. The Word of God together with the water of baptism had adopted us into such a Spiritual family. Such wonders never cease for those who walk by faith.

America's Dairyland and a Dad who did it his way!

Wisconsin is known as America's Dairyland. Our family represented that in two ways: (1) Dad had a dairy farm and (2) eventually also owned a small cheese factory. Dad was an enterprising individual. When the money was short, he didn't complain. He became more creative. He'd plant a larger garden, raise more cows, or pigs, or poultry. He did not complain about paying taxes either. For example, he would say, "It's cheaper for me to pay taxes than to buy all the equipment needed to keep roads repaired, snow plowed in winter, and if ever needed for an emergency, a fire truck."

Eventually, Dad began hauling milk for the local cheese factory manager in order to earn more money to raise his family, now five children. Soon he was also employed as a worker within the factory, became a licensed cheese maker, and eventually was put in charge as manager so the owner could go elsewhere to manage a larger operation across the river in Minnesota. Through an unforeseen circumstance, Dad rallied the patrons who sold milk to that factory enterprise. He asked them, "Would you support me as manager of this factory if I borrow the money to assure you of the back pay that you have coming." Evidently the patrons said, "Yes."

Something had happened through the previous proprietorship which left two options: (1) conduct an auction and divide the proceeds amongst the farmers. Although they would probably not receive the fair financial return they were entitled too. (2) Dad (or someone) could borrow the money to assure the farmer patrons of the money they were expecting. That otherwise potentially very negative circumstance, turned into a positive outcome for those farmers and my father. Thanks to his willingness to risk and to invest love and labor at that historic moment, for the next decade plus a few more years, my father became a dairy plant owner/operator. That involved a good deal of interaction with the public including inspectors who showed up unexpectedly on behalf of the State. Occasionally these inspectors, probably with all good intentions, had contradictory recommendations. Occasionally my father's response was to confront these authorities with their contradictory expectations. Observing that example served me well in situations to be shared later in this writing.

While the classroom provides a wonderful learning laboratory, everyday life experience (sometimes called the school of hard knocks) also provides wisdom for many life situations. While yet in high school, Dad arranged for me, his oldest son of five children, (Sonia was the oldest, Mavis, Forrest and Bruce were younger in that order) to come a few minutes late for morning class so that I could haul one load of milk before driving to school in my 1937 Ford. Milk hauling was a physical fitness exercise in the days of milk cans weighing one hundred pounds when filled. Thankfully most of them were not filled to the top. I was totally unaware at

3

the time of how these accumulating experiences were helping to shape me for the role of pastor I've shared now for
almost fifty years.

Sometimes when I feel weary, I remember those
days of running into a farmer's milk house and grabbing one
or two cans of milk and rushing to the truck, loading them,
then driving off to try and impress my father with how
quickly I had completed that milk route.

Shortly after graduating from high school my father
sent me to Winter Dairy School at the University of Wisconsin so that I'd become a licensed Wisconsin cheese maker.

In the process of manufacturing cheese from the
milk provided by the farmers, there's a stage at which thousands of pounds of milk becomes a vat full of cheese curds
before the final stages of the cheese making process when
the curds were pressed into a solid mold and held in that
form overnight for later sale to the public. Occasionally
tourists would stop in to buy the cheese curds for their eating enjoyment.

That factory was located on the corner of Highway
#27, which then connected Osseo, Wisconsin, with the
county seat of Jackson County, Black River Falls. As Dad's
helper one day, I had an *unforgettable spiritual awakening*
that has been a life directing experience to this present time
in my life—that story with more details comes later.

Incidentally, that church building with the elegant
steeple is located one mile to the east of the cheese factory.
To this present day that building is a kind of sacramental
sign to me. Certainly, we can worship Almighty God without
a building, but that place did help prepare me to have reverence for that very special book, the Bible.

Our family had one pastor, a Gospel-centered
preacher, Rev. E.B. Christopherson, for fifty-four years. He
served three rural congregations and began a fourth in approximately his forty-fifth year of ministry. Another meas-
ure of his stature is that he served on the board of regents of
the University of Wisconsin. He was also somewhat well

known for his herd of excellent dairy cattle; besides pastoring those congregations. What a combination of talents and interests! Our family had regular connections with him and that place where he served as our pastor.

One humorous story told about him is of a day he was walking out of a local tavern with a six pack of beer. One man made a comment about a pastor carrying a six pack of beer. As the story was told, the Reverend Pastor set the six pack of beer down and picked the man up with his hands so they were eye ball to eye ball and said before setting him back down, "You're just a little boy in my hands, young man." The pastor then left the tavern. Another humorous story was about my Uncle Marv, quite a heavy drinker, who was heard singing hymns among the crowd at Lake Martha Days, a local annual celebration, the pastor then said to him, "Sure glad you haven't forgotten everything your mother taught you."

On an otherwise normal afternoon while alone in the factory and cleaning the equipment at the end of the day, I felt an overwhelming compulsion to get my hands on a Bible. At that moment, I remembered mother kept her Sunday School teaching materials in a basket under her bed, so I rushed up the stairs to the apartment, opened her Bible and read a few words. My older sister at a recent family gathering remembered that day. She remembers I rushed up stairs asking, "Where's Mother's Bible?"

While reading a few words in Mother's Bible, the Holy Spirit spoke to me in a mysterious way I'd never experienced. While not having yet the vocabulary to interpret that moment in the same way I do now, there was an inner voice that said, "Before you get married, before you choose a vocation, before you make any major decisions concerning your future, you must get better acquainted with this book, the Bible." At that moment, my parents arrived home. I heard the car enter the driveway. Without telling them of that most unusual mental/emotional/spiritual experience, I returned the Bible to its place and rushed back to my duties in the factory. Looking back, it now reminds me of that voice St. Augustine is said to have heard in the garden, the voice which said, "Take up and read." That voice sent him to the Bible, and he read a portion of Romans 13 which helped create that new trajectory for his life.

"Long ago God spoke to our ancestors in many and various ways by the prophets, …" (Hebrews 1:1); and he continues to speak today to persons receptive to his message of eternal friendship through the mission and meaning of the cross.

Military draft was a daunting reality for young men in those days, the 1950s. If you didn't enlist in the military, you could be drafted at any time—even well into adulthood. Therefore, it was my considered decision to enlist in the military. Typically, then as now, one had to choose which branch of the Service to enter so I chose the Marine Corps with its reputation for discipline.

While reviewing and reflecting upon that decision, I'm led to believe that Jesus, the Christ, was strengthening me as written on the plaque Mother had hung on our bedroom wall. Choosing the Marine Corps was also, due in part (I now believe), to fragments of conversations overheard among family and relatives which were lingering in my mind. One portion of such a conversation concerned a man who came out of the military as an alcoholic. Those stories sometimes related to how much booze one could drink and still walk straight.

Another image of adulthood (manhood) was of an ex-military man of such coarseness, that as I recall, he loved to fight and it was said of him, "He probably wouldn't shed a tear at his mother's funeral." In our family culture, those kind of examples were mentioned with deep concern and as behaviors to be avoided. Such images, I recall, were not examples of manhood I, nor my parents respected. Those thoughts influenced my decision to join a branch of military with a reputation for toughness and try to come through the experience with compassion and character intact. Such

6

choices, I believe, were the result of conversations over-heard around the family table—probably mostly at meal time—a treasured time lapse memory from those growing up years. Thanks be to Almighty God, I had wonderful examples of integrity around me in relatives, neighbors, and other acquaintances, which continue to inspire gratitude.

But I was challenged. I was learning that life is full of choices that could propel one onto that narrow way that leads to life, or the other way that leads to destruction (Matthew 7:13-14). Choices determine and outline one's future.

Stories of deep regret are regular testimonies of persons who have travelled the journey of addiction and by the grace of God were awakened to the new reality of living without drugs or alcohol. It's not unusual to hear someone say at one of their Narcotic Anonymous (NA) meetings, "I'm glad that I ended up in jail because it gave me a new perspective on my life and helped deliver me from dependence upon chemicals to cope with life's challenges." Bible Studies in jails and prisons are a great resource to awaken and refocus the life of some persons addicted to drugs and/or alcohol. Occasionally I like to tell the story of Chuck Colson who was sent to prison on a charge related to the Watergate scandal. While in prison and participating in Bible Study he became a Christian. Upon release he started prison ministries in many countries.

My heart goes out to persons incarcerated and; therefore, I assist with an afternoon Sunday Worship Service at the local jail. Also, most Saturday nights I attend an NA meeting, not because I'm an addict; but to learn more about the experience of addicts from the stories of NA members. The path into addiction to alcohol and/or drugs (getting and staying clean) is filled with choices. In the area where I live there are at least twenty-one NA/AA meetings each week where folks gather to support and encourage one another. What a gift those meetings become for those who attend them and practice the principles outlined and reviewed at each meeting before the sharing of personal stories.

If the branch of the military I chose wasn't of stern reputation, (so I thought at that time) and I was by the grace of God, able to come through that with compassion and character intact (not an addict or with other afflictions), then no one could say, "But if you had joined this or that branch it might have been different."

While driving Dad's milk truck from farm to farm and back to unload at the factory, thoughts on the consequences of choices were churning in my mind. To this day I ask myself over and over again with great reverence, "Where did such noble thoughts come from at such a young age?" The answer I give myself is that it's the work of the Holy Spirit in answer to prayers and the influences of parents and many others.

Conditioned by such a secure, loving home environment with the added reinforcement of spiritual powers (check out Ephesians 6 in the New Testament of the Bible) appreciation for spiritual realities had increased.

Incidentally, when going out and returning to the Cheese Factory with the milk truck, I regularly passed that elegant church building mentioned above. The sight always stirs my emotions; not only the building but more importantly what it represents. It became a joke among some folks to say, "See you in church if you sit by the window." For us who quite often were required to work on Sundays that was reality—especially if driving a truck past the building with people at worship.

Therein lies the purpose of this book, that is, to document once again, the reality of spiritual guidance, spiritual promise, and Presence. Our Lord commends that awesome biblical truth for all people. Proverbs 3:5-6 is a great counsel for parents and everyone else: "Trust in the Lord with all your heart and do not rely on your own understanding. In all your ways acknowledge Him and He will make your paths straight." "I can do all things through Christ who strengthens me" (Philippians 4:13). Thankfully, I can also say with conviction in the words of Romans 1:16-17, "I am not ashamed of the Gospel for it is the power of God unto salvation for the Jew first and also to the Gentile for in it the righteousness of God is revealed through faith for faith."

The marvels of spiritual life have parallels in the marvel of our physical life. Professor Anthony A. Goodman, M.D. shares these words in his book *Understanding the Human Body*.

"We have a heart that pumps 1.3 gallons of blood per minute, approximately 700,000 gallons per year. Those figures are for a body at rest and much more when the body is active" (Professor Anthony A. Goodman, M.D. F.A.C.S. is adjunct professor in the Department of Microbiology at Montana State University, P. 4, *Understanding the Human Body: An Introduction to Anatomy and Physiology*, Great Courses Guidebook).

If we can function daily without thinking about how awesomely wonderful is physical life, so also we can do that regarding the awesome gift of faith and how it becomes a functioning reality. "By faith we understand that the worlds were prepared by the word of God, so that what is seen is made from things that are not visible" (Hebrews 11:3). The more we know about nano technology, the more awesome that Bible passage becomes; "so faith comes from what is heard and what is heard comes through the word of Christ" (Romans 10:17).

Brennan Manning, in his book *The Ragamuffin Gospel*, has these words also pointing to the awesomeness of the physical world. "The world's weight has been estimated at six sextillion tons (that's a six with 21 zeros). Yet it is perfectly balanced and turns easily on its axis. It revolves daily at a rate of more than 1,000 miles per hour or 25,000 miles

each day. Considering the tremendous weight of six sextillion tons rolling at this fantastic speed around an invisible
axis held in place by unseen bands of gravitation, the words
of Job 26:7 take on unparalleled significance, "He poised the
earth on nothingness." (*The Ragamuffin Gospel*, Brennan
Manning, Multinomah Publishers, Inc., 1990, 2000).

We marvel at the spiritual realities of life. In our
Christian understanding of life, the same awesome Creator
has given us both.

CHAPTER TWO
An Awesome Motivation

"For everything there is a season, and a time for every matter under heaven (Ecclesiastes 3:1).

After a relatively happy childhood and a busy first twenty years of life, a new spiritual reality began influencing my decisions in increasingly significant ways. It was the urgent feeling as never before to hold and read the Bible. When I opened the Bible randomly to what page I've never remembered; but have never forgotten the stirring reality that spoke to me and said, "Before you get married, before you choose what you are going to do with the rest of your life, you must get better acquainted with this book."

Life up to this time had been lived among our family of five children, two girls and three boys. Those early years had been devoted to chores on the farm with supervision by a loving father and mother, attending three different one-room country schools, and finishing the required four years of high school at Lincoln Hill High School in Osseo, Wisconsin.

That mention of high school triggered a memory of a visit to the University of Wisconsin, Eau Claire, when I was a senior. The comment of one of the speakers raised a strong emotional reaction in me. That speaker made a point of saying, "Unless you are at least in the upper half of your class academically, you perhaps should not consider going on to college. Somewhere from within my psyche came a rebellious thought, like, "Who in the H ... do you think you are to tell me whether or not I should go on to college?" While I didn't say that aloud, it was simply a thought in mind. What surprises me about that moment in hindsight, is the realization at that time in my life, to the best of my knowledge now, I had no intention of going to college. So it seems to me that impulsive thought was the Holy Spirit counseling me not to let such sentiments condition my aspirations for the future.

Working with my father at that time in my life was such a high priority that I would have quit high school except that my mother would not hear of it; and, Dad would probably have approved that I quit, after all he dropped out of school at a young age—I believe before his freshmen year in high school.

I do not recall my standing within my high school class academically, and at that point I didn't really much care because Dad had me so involved in the business culture. He even had me attend a bookkeeping course at the University of Wisconsin, Eau Claire Campus to help in handling the business management details of his business.

After high school came a relatively active social life. In that rural Wisconsin culture, the dance halls were frequented by family, friends and neighbors. In those days, because of family, friends and neighbors in those places you were never there alone among strangers. That fact served as a social safety net. That probably curbed some behaviors that could have been harmful because friends, family, and neighbors would probably be the first to know.

With sisters somewhat insistent that this brother know how to dance, I remember some of their dance lessons for me around the dining room table in our home. A local grocery clerk, when she heard that I was planning to become a pastor, exclaimed, "Then he will not be able to dance anymore." Whether that's true or not I can say, very honestly, "But now I have something much more rewarding and fulfilling to do."

The strong impulses and emotions of that Spiritual Awakening never left me, although it happened at about age twenty. Today that moment calls to mind those words of Jesus, "The Spirit blows where it chooses..." (John 3:8). Walls and doors and roofs and ceilings could not prevent the Spirit's entrance. That experience became a lighthouse along the way for many future decisions. Often the words "I can do all things through him" (Philippians 4:13) consoles, comforts and motivates me.

The military draft was active in those days, and I had been contemplating fulfilling my obligation to that calling. Once that big decision day arrived, it was time to pack up and leave home. Mother had packed a Gideon New Testament and my Confirmation Bible as they were preparing to accompany me, their second oldest child to the train depot in LaCrosse, Wisconsin. (At that point I'm not sure Mother had been told about my resolve to search the scriptures with every spare moment during military duty.) Mother was a prayer warrior. She probably would have felt blessed to know the resolve I felt to better understand the meaning of the biblical revelation she had so diligently been living and teaching. As this is written, I'm reminded that knowing more now of the workings of the Holy Spirit than I did then, she may have been given some assurance of that resolve without me having mentioned it to her. Though I'm quite sure I didn't share with her those new wonders of grace at work in my life; nevertheless, her prayers for me, and certainly for her other children, were being richly blessed.

Aboard the train in LaCrosse, Wisconsin, with parents waving to me at departure time, I was on my way to San Diego Marine Corps Boot Camp. Another passenger in that part of the train, a Mr. Stickney, invited me to play a card game. That was a test, and the first of many decisions to follow the resolve to search the Scriptures. I declined that invitation in favor of another value, to read the New Testament on that train trip west. Oh, how beautiful the quiet work of the Holy Spirit! Even though I grew up in a card playing family, at this point in my life the Holy Spirit was pointing me into another use of my time. As a young person, I can remember rollicking laughter among adults enjoying card club gatherings in our farm home—while we children in the upstairs bedroom were supposed to be asleep.

Boot Camp at Camp Pendleton in San Diego was relatively uneventful and routine except that one highlight was mail call, at least once a week. Every week I received a letter from my mother, so faithful was she in remembering to write to me. Approximately forty young men during Boot Camp sat in anticipation at each mail call. Some received no mail; however, due to such a devout mother, my name was always called and a letter from home always passed on to me. Another value and reward received because of devout caring parents! Her weekly letters to me continued throughout those nearly three years in the military. What a consolation, news from home, and a tangible gesture of caring from home.

One morning I'd had the 4 o'clock to 8 o'clock guard duty, so it was my responsibility to waken the platoon at a certain time. Guess I was feeling a bit mischievous or giddy at the moment, so I took the bayonet from my belt and hit the jacket around the heater in the barracks at the same time I yelled, "Reveille!" At that moment, every blanket on the bunks of that barracks flew into the air. Obviously, I got their attention. Private Sims, the platoon leader, a rather large, physically fit fellow, came over to me and said something like, "Don't you ever do that again." His presence was such that I perceived him as a person of fine character; therefore, I was not greatly disturbed by his threat. As the platoon leader, he was within his rights to counsel me. And, since that duty was passed around among the platoon recruits, that opportunity never came to me again.

During Boot Camp, came another surprise as my name was called one day at noon to lead our platoon from the chow hall back to the barracks. That consisted of marching alongside of the other forty plus recruits and calling the cadence: one, two, three, four. I've often reflected on "Why Me?" It was an honor, of course. (Incidentally, whenever a promotion time came along, this simple farm boy received the promotion, even up to sergeant by the time of discharge in less than three years.) After Boot Camp came the required four weeks of Advanced Infantry Training at Oceanside, California.

While downtown Oceanside on some off-duty hours, I became aware of the Christian Business Men's Club. Those Christian businessmen were interested in befriending military persons and providing them with Christian fellowship while so many of us were far from home. How thoughtful: one more of the beautiful ways our Lord continues to nurture and bless his people. Someone had to come up with that inspired idea; others had to follow through.

One day while sitting at the food bar within that Christian Business Men's Center, I became aware of a Bible Study in another room and decided to attend. At that Bible Study, such a blessing came into my consciousness that in retrospect, I felt at that moment anointed to teach the Bible.

On that occasion, I did not have the maturity or vocabulary to characterize it as such, but looking back now, that's what I've come to believe. When I walked away from that Bible Study, I felt some new motivation and purpose had entered my life. Even as I write these words fifty plus years later, I can vividly remember that special feeling. It was an uplifting, reassuring experience, but with no hint at that point of how that would play out into the future. However, later chapters will illustrate how that moment of inspiration has been unfolding through the years. Today there's absolutely nothing I'd rather do than study the greatest book ever written and prepare homilies and Bible Studies for the several opportunities I have to do that each week. At a recent Bible study, the words of Psalm 111:2 have become a favorite

Bible passage to ponder, "The Lord's words are great, studied by all who delight in them" (Holman Christian Standard Bible).

We pray in public worship and at other times and places for the Lord God to call persons into the pastoral ministry. Every person has his or her own story of how that Call entered their life.

While preparing for worship, I occasionally pick the following words to be sung by the community gathered for worship. These following words on the Holy Spirit express a truth by which we are called and guided into various vocations to serve.

"Holy Spirit, truth divine, dawn upon this soul of mine;
Breath of God and inward light, wake my spirit,
clear my sight."
In stanza three: "Holy Spirit, power divine, fortify this will
of mine; by your will I strongly live, bravely bear,
and nobly strive.

Either at that juncture in time, or after Sea Duty and back to Oceanside, I was at a service center playing table tennis with a person whom I had just met. We decided to attend a movie. While sitting in the movie, his hand began roving over my thigh. We had been warned that any homosexual activity (and person) would be severely reprimanded. At the moment (pondering my duty and how to respond), I decided to follow military orders. I excused myself with the excuse of needing to go to the restroom; but instead I called the military police. They arrived, sat down behind us in the theater, and soon marched that man out of the theater. Knowing something of military disciplines, I realize now I may have caused him to be dishonorably discharged. At the time, I was proud of doing my duty as a Marine as I then thought I understood it. Through the years however, I have become more aware of so much heartache, and too much judgementalism on the lesbian, gay, bisexual, transgender issues that I no longer feel the same about reporting that person to the Military Police. Now I wish I'd have been wiser and more helpful to that young man.

Once again it was decision time, a choice to sign up for Sea Duty as a Marine Detachment aboard ship with a large majority of Navy personnel, or to remain an infantry Marine. Since it was peacetime (1956), though I wanted to maintain my commitment to be in the most disciplined section of the military, as I understood that at the time (an infantry Marine). Sea Duty, on the other hand, would provide travel to different parts of the world. In peacetime, an infantry Marine would probably remain in the States, so I signed up for Sea Duty and ended up aboard the USS Philippine Sea CVS 47, an aircraft carrier with a squadron of propeller planes.

CHAPTER THREE
Life Aboard Ship (One Marine's Experience)

"From ages past no one has heard, no ear has perceived, no eye has seen any God besides you, who works for those who wait for him" (Isaiah 64:4). "No testing has overtaken you that is not common to everyone. God is faithful, and he will not let you be tested beyond your strength, but with the testing he will also provide the way out so that you may be able to endure it"
(1 Corinthians 10:13).

Marines served aboard aircraft carriers, cruiser ships and destroyers. Marines were assigned to be orderlies for the ship's captain, and co-captain and to provide guards for the ship's incarcerated. Also, Marines were to provide maintenance on the gun mounts of the ship; and when needed to form the nucleus for the ship's landing party.

There I was aboard the aircraft carrier USS Philippine Sea, CVS 47, a farm boy and dairy plant worker whose father also made sure I went to winter dairy school in Madison, Wisconsin, to become a licensed cheese maker. And now I was in an entirely different culture at approximately twenty-one years of age, one among twenty-two hundred Military Navy personnel. Approximately sixty of the twenty-two hundred were Marines. Though an interracial environment, I had never talked—so far as I recall, to a person of another race.

Our ship was almost immediately called upon to rescue bodies floating in the water due to the crash of an air transport plane shortly after leaving an airport in Hawaii.

Rescued bodies were spread out on the hanger deck of the ship. Some were shark eaten so that only the bones were visible. When I hear of a plane crashing at sea, that horrific scene comes back to mind.

We Marines had our own barracks with bunk beds, stacked two high, and I had a lower bunk. There was a social area with coffee pots, a table and perhaps a fridge; but I did not spend much time there. When not on duty, I was in my bunk reading Scripture. My Confirmation Bible remains thoroughly underlined with thoughts written into the margins. So I became labeled as a Bible reading person; but gratefully did develop some nice friendships.

Several other experiences aboard that ship flood my memory from time to time. Among them, I vividly recall the day I was doing my assigned duty on gun mount maintenance and a tall robust corporal began hounding (bullying) me as to the way I was swabbing the deck. As I submitted to that briefly, it gradually occurred to me that as a relatively new Marine aboard ship and lesser rank than that bullying corporal, would I, should I, submit to that kind of bullying for the remainder of my tour of duty? So I thought we may as well handle this right now. The simple logic I applied to the situation went something like: here I am a new person aboard ship with most of seventeen months to serve. Rather than put up with this all that time and what that might do to my character and self-esteem, I chose another value—I'd rather be in the ship's jail than be subjected to such bullying for the duration.

Some of this spunky decision making may have come from watching my father deal with State Inspectors in the Wisconsin Cheese Factory – as those inspectors often had contradictory expectations and Dad did not restrain himself from calling that to their attention. Seldom do we realize at the time the long-range affects certain daily experiences may have upon our future.

Looking up at this corporal, higher rank, and much more robust than I, I said, "My intention is to do a thorough and proper job of swabbing this deck. When I'm done, if it's not good enough, tell me and I'll do it again; but while I'm doing this, leave me alone; or you can take this swab and shove it down your throat." In response, he made a pronouncement about my future aboard that ship and then stomped off the gun mount. At that very moment I heard a whistle to come over to a hatch through which that encounter had been observed by a higher-ranking Navy officer who said, "If you get any discipline for that, let me know. That corporal had no business treating you as he did." Fact is that issue never came up again and after one other incident, which we clarified with a brief discussion, we became friends.

That moment aboard ship takes on greater significance now as I recall so much emphasis in the news of children and youth being bullied in school settings. In high school one fellow attempted to bully me and an upper classman stepped in and warned him to stop it or else. Bullying never happened again to me in high school—or since, until this time in the military. Oh, how I hope there's always some such person to intervene on behalf of others who might be bullied at any stage in their life experience. That not only is humiliating, but can also change one's character and personality.

That same evening, however, with that bullying experience fresh in my mind, that corporal kicked a poster board of the list of the ship's landing party. The poster was hanging on a set of steel lockers. That kick could be heard throughout the Marine quarters, and that is probably what the big corporal intended. He also made the loud statement, "It looks like it's only the 'shit birds' who are not on the landing party list."

So, I checked the list and noted my name was not on the list. Thinking he was referring to me, in view of our afternoon encounter, I went to him and said as he stood in the corner by his bunk, "Are you calling me a '__ bird' since my name is not on that list. He stood silent for a moment and

21

then said, "No, I was referring to myself, my name is not on that list either." From that moment on we became friends.

A few months later our ship was docked at a port in Japan. Evidently it was a usual practice for so-called leaders for certain social activities to contact houses of ill repute—better known as places of prostitution—to line up dates between willing shipboard persons and those practicing that whore work. It was also a revelation to this naïve farm boy, to notice that tables of medications were also made available by the gang plank (entrance/exit) to the ship, while in port, to help offset the effects of sexually transmitted diseases and other diseases that could be contracted in that different cultural setting.

Since I didn't sign up for the so-called party in the bar, fellow marines gathered around me on another gun mount, and told me that they had just the right prostitute and just the right place lined up for me, and that I should join them because I just didn't know how much fun I was missing. With perfect peace I could say to them, "Fellows, you don't know what you are missing by not knowing Jesus Christ as your Savior and Lord." They just looked at each other, shook their heads, and walked away and never again brought up that topic to me. Once again my Lord and His Word had delivered me. "No testing has overtaken you, that is not common to everyone" (1 Corinthians 10:13).

One of those party guys, later regretted having passed on a sexually transmitted disease to his wife while home on leave. Sin, for example the commandment on adultery does have its consequences.

Mother Remembers

Mother had occasionally mentioned that a distant cousin, and his wife, were missionaries in Japan. It became one goal of mine to see them if possible since I'd be in that vicinity. So when our ship was docked at a Japan port, I caught a train to make the trip to see that missionary family. On the way, I needed to stay overnight at a hotel. At the hotel, I was escorted to my room by one of the hotel staff. As we were approaching the room in which I would stay for the night, he escorted me past a large room with the door wide open—making sure I looked into that room in which several women (seems they'd appropriately be called prostitutes) were lying there bare naked. So why take me past such a scene? The first guess might be that a desire for that kind of company could have yielded a monetary reward for the hotel owner, or to whomever, for the required fee. What a blatant disregard for the consequences of such shoddy morality!

How ironic in retrospect that I was on my way to visit missionaries who were there to share the Gospel with its moral expectations; and on the way I'm reminded of that alternative life style. Such forces of temptation exist in so many places around the world, ready to lure even the most precious child/youth into that environment. It's a troubling reality to me that the media so boldly presents suggestive behavioral images, with the most elegant of artistic décor, but stops short of explaining the longer-range consequences of many behaviors displayed. Children, youth and many adults without appropriate wisdom gained through training and mentoring can too easily be misled by those millions of dollars spent to influence their behaviors. Those persons suffer the consequences and society ends up paying the financial debt incurred.

Now I ponder how the Lord may have been guiding to help achieve his moral and spiritual purposes. "No testing has overtaken you that is not common to everyone. God is faithful, and he will not let you be tested beyond your strength, but with the testing he will also provide the way out so that you may be able to endure it" (1 Corinthians 10:13). Incidentally, in regard to the visit with the missionaries I would like to have learned more about their experience of serving in that Japanese culture than I did. Seems I encountered them at a very busy time.

23

These years later we keep in touch with YWAM (Youth With A Mission) missionaries who serve in Mongolia, and we have a few other such contacts who help us appreciate the challenge of serving in a culture different from America. More on YWAM later.

Sometime later aboard that ship, while walking past the administrative office, Darwin asked me whether I'd ever had any typing experience. Honestly, I had to answer, "Very little, one course in high school; but I'd appreciate a chance for more experience." He answered, "I'm going on leave and need someone to take my place in the office." So for the thirty days during his leave, I was an administrative assistant aboard ship sharing a small office with the master sergeant of that marine detachment. When Darwin returned from leave, evidently the first sergeant thought that I was doing all right so Darwin said, "I'm being discharged soon so you may as well continue in the office." Now I had my own private office after hours to continue my Bible Study and prayers. That fit so well with my earlier resolve to pursue a more thorough understanding of Our Lord's precious word: "the Lord works for them who wait for him" (Isaiah 64:4).

One recurring vision happened while sitting in that office, even as the ship was rocking on the high seas of the Pacific Ocean, that vision was of the picture over the altar in that Country Church back home: the picture is of Jesus reaching out to Peter's cry, "Lord, save me!" (Matthew 14:30). It is interesting how childhood memories and Christian nurture were connecting there in the Pacific Ocean all those miles from my Country Church. Even while aboard the moving ship thousands of miles west, I received inspiration from that steeple adorned Country Church.

In a devotional book, *Breakfast for the Soul*, devotion 43 is titled "God's Mysterious Guidance" by Christian psychologist, Paul Tournier. He begins that devotion with this quote from George Washington, "Providence has at all times been my only dependence, for all other resources seem to have failed us." Tournier continues his devotion as follows: "God guides us, despite our uncertainties and vagueness, even through our failings and mistakes" (Honor Books, 1946, p. 108). Mysterious Guidance is a great theme of Scripture and the lives of Christians.

Another of several rewards of having my private get-away office aboard ship was that in the evenings after the day's work, fellow Marines, knowing my convictions, would stop by to share some of their personal story. Even the corporal previously mentioned would stop for an evening visit.

There came a time for another party in port. Now the first sergeant made it clear he expected all of his marine detachment to participate in the party at another lounge/bar on land. So I (we) felt trapped, you don't normally go against the will of your first sergeant. Well, we did! The "we" includes my fellow office worker Melvin who had recently married and vowed to be faithful to his wife. He also happened to be of the Christian Scientist confession of faith. Melvin became another gift in the right place at the right time for me; and perhaps I for him.

Together we agreed that we would not attend the party. Then the first sergeant, after hearing our resolve, said placing his hands (I can still see his hands in my mind's eye) on the bottom half of the door that was closed as he said emphatically, "All right, then you will both be the military police at the party." So we were! I've never been to a party like that before or since!

One of my duties was to rouse a man and his prostitute partner, probably too drunk to realize they were in the wrong room, from his slumbers so he could move to another room. He had vomited straight up and the vomit formed around his chin and neck. I can still see that vomit crumbling around his face. Soon the party was over. Evidently, we managed to perform our duties adequately, and life moved on without any further consequences on those issues. Those kind of parties for which we were expected to be military police, seem to be expected social behaviors. It takes some boldness to resist such peer pressure. In the words of the Bible verse at the head of this chapter "God is faithful and will provide a way of escape."

Where I grew up in rural Wisconsin, as mentioned, I could not remember talking to a person of another color. Now aboard ship I spent some time working out in the ship's gym with a person of color, probably African-American. One day after that fellow just mentioned had become "Runner Up" for the Mr. Hawaii body builders, he stopped by the Marine quarters and said, with some jest while flexing his muscles, "If any of you pick on that Olson fellow" (that's me), "remember you'll have to deal with me too." We shared not only the gym workout experience, but also reverence for the message of the Bible and the new life possibilities revealed therein. Another sign of the protection which follows me "...all the days of my life..." (Psalm 23:6).

I took a few lessons in boxing, however, at night I caught myself lying in my bunk practicing boxing tactics and decided that I did not want my mind to be preoccupied with that. Boxing is consuming physically, emotionally and mentally. Getting hurt is both physical and emotional. Making all the right moves, defensively and offensively, requires lots of mental energy. While grateful for a few things I learned, other priorities seemed more important—so I discontinued that involvement.

The USS Philippine Sea just happened to be in the right place at the time to be a prop for the movie, "Wings of an Eagle" with John Wayne. In the movie, he is transferred from a cruiser onto the USS Philippine Sea. We Marines were to be the Honor Guard to welcome him. In the movie, I can find myself way in the back row as part of the Honor Guard.

We had some informal conversation with John Wayne that day and he signed some autographs. Someone asked him if he ever tired of signing autographs and he responded, "Hell, no, I'm just worried about the day when no one wants my autograph." Occasionally I have some fun telling someone that the only movie I ever appeared in was with

John Wayne. That always gets a quizzical look and gives me a chance to tell that story.

During this time, my rank changed from private first class to corporal. As that seventeen months aboard ship were winding down (thankfully, I had gotten to set foot on the soil of several countries), a conviction was growing in me that I was being Called by the Holy Spirit into some full-time Christian ministry. At the end of the seventeen months, I was transferred from the ship to a military base in Oceanside, California. My MOS, Military Occupational Specialty, by this time had become administrative assistant, rather than simply "rifleman."

Now my duty was at a desk in a rather large office with approximately a dozen other persons of various ranks. It happened that one Major was a witnessing Christian, which was a comfort to me. He kept a Bible on his desk, and we had some Christian sharing conversations.

Another learning experience in that setting was that card playing for money was a favorite pastime at the end of the work day and on occasion someone would lose their next pay check to pay their gambling debt. That was one of several experiences in my life, going back even to black jack gambling at the back of the school bus for pennies. Mother issued her warnings to me against the dangers of gambling. In one congregation, I served, a high school boy who wanted to farm the home place was prevented from doing that because his father lost the farm in a gambling ring in that small Iowa town.

As I thank Almighty God for the counsel of Christian parents, I grieve for the erosion of the family and the sordid scenes of the media that mislead children and youth. Recently at Narcotics Anonymous group, which I attend because they meet weekly in the Chapel of First Lutheran, a Waterloo, Iowa, congregation where Ella and I serve, I asked the group, "Tell me how you recall that the advertising of liquor affected your ability to recover from your addiction."

One of the participants quickly responded, and later another, on how subtle such an advertising message became a hindrance to recovery. The message that evening in the *Just for Today Book* was that addiction is not a hopeless journey; but a treatable disease. As a participant at those meetings, I try to reinforce that new understanding of addiction: addiction as a disease is evidence-based science now—not just a matter of will power as in the old-school way of thinking that said alcoholics and drug addicts just need to toughen up and say, "No." Addicts who are now clean know that they need the group NA or AA, and a Higher Power to stay clean; it's not *just* a matter of will power. Colorful pictures can be displayed of the brain change difference under the influence of addiction to drugs and/or alcohol.

During this time with Military duty winding down, during off hours, I attended evangelism crusades and answered a few altar calls. Gradually, it dawned on me that putting that decision into action was more important than walking to that altar over and over again.

In a letter to Mother, I indicated my conviction that I was feeling called into full-time Christian ministry. Thinking that I was not worthy of being a pastor, I had done some research and decided to attend Prairie Bible Institute in Canada. Not knowing what opportunities might be available, I thought, perhaps I could be a maintenance man at a Mission Station.

Mother convinced me to go instead to Luther College in Decorah, Iowa, which school our family pastor had attended. So I applied and was accepted. "Honor your father and your mother," a part of that moral code of the Christian faith, again proved so valuable. Would my father be disappointed that his first-born son would not be joining him in his dairy business? That really was my intention when I enlisted in the military—to get the military obligation satisfied and settle in working with my dad. While on leave near the end of my three-year military obligation, I broke the news to Dad that I felt Called into, possibly the pastoral ministry, his answer—as I recall was, "I will sell every cow on the place to put you through seminary if that's what it takes." Dad evidently still had the farm with cows along with the cheese factory business. (Incidentally, he did not have to sell anything to put me through college.)

In those days, one could be discharged up to three months early if one had been accepted at a college, in order to make the start date for a semester. Even after achieving the rank of sergeant, I was discharged early to make that semester start at Luther College the fall of 1958.

CHAPTER FOUR
College, Catfish, Classics and Courtship

"Do your best to present yourself to God as one approved by him, a worker who has no need to be ashamed, rightly explaining the word of truth" (2 Timothy 2:15).

A divine protection incident happened on the way home from the military, while driving my 1949 Studebaker, which I had purchased in California. While driving through Montana on its long, straight highways, there appeared in the distance, a man walking along, gloves sticking out of his back pocket, whom I wrongly perceived to be a person with a stalled car just over the next hill on the road. So, I offered him a ride. Once in my car beside me, he stated that his motorcycle had broken down miles back and he simply left it, because he wanted to get to a certain place further east to look for a job.

Seeing my Bible beside me, he began some pious conversation with me. During those conversations, I began to think that he was a committed Christian man. With that conviction, and wanting a job, and knowing my dad was always looking for someone who would do an honest day's work for a fair wage, I offered to take him home with me. Mother said sometime later, "I had a feeling Gary would bring someone home with him." Incidentally, I had not seen my parents since my last leave home from the military.

It was only a few days before I had to register for the freshman year at Luther College so I had time to spend with my "hitchhiker" new acquaintance. I began to question the character of my new acquaintance when I noticed that he was more interested in playing with my younger brother out there in the field, than working diligently as he had tried to impress upon me that he would. Jumping ahead in the story, my ever faithful Mother continued writing to me while at college. It became obvious through her letters that the person I had brought home had become a nuisance. Rather than the positive inspirational force I'd hoped he would be, my hitchhiker acquaintance became a distraction and a worrisome burden.

Dad had offered to buy him new clothes and buy him a ticket on a bus to wherever he wanted to go—just to get him off the farm and out of the community. So, my hitchhiker friend was sent on his way. Dad never chastised me for bringing that man to his farm. His fatherly wisdom and compassion seemingly chalked it up to a lesson well learned by all.

In one of her later letters, Mother told of being home alone one day when a motorcycle pulled into the yard. She recognized the rider as that fellow I had brought home with me. She called the neighbors to inform my father who was assisting that neighbor. By the time he came home, that motorcycle and rider had left the yard. (Sometime prior to that day, that fellow whom Dad had sent away, had come back on a cycle at chore time wondering if the men on chore duty could help him repaint his motor cycle.) Had he stolen the cycle? I don't know. By this time, red flags were flying in my father's mind, too. He began to investigate and discovered that when I picked up this man in Montana, he had probably just been released from prison.

By the time my father returned in response to my mother's call, the guy on the motorcycle was gone from the yard. Filled with suspicion as to who and what this person was doing back in the territory, Dad rushed into town (Osseo, Wisconsin) and noticed him fueling his motor cycle at a gas station. He notified the police and said, "Please arrest this man." Can't remember now which jail we last heard he had been sentenced to—but we heard no more of him. An investigation evidently revealed continued criminal behavior.

Other Choices

While continuing at Luther College a choice came along as to whether to play football. Though I'd never been a serious athlete, I gave it a try. I soon realized that a choice had to be made between studies and at least "B" grades, or football. The choice was a "no brainer," and I can remember that day walking off the field with the shoulder pads slung over my shoulders acting on that choice clearly realizing that I was prioritizing my values for the future. (As a matter of fact, I probably would not have excelled in the game of football anyway.)

Life is filled with choices. Once in a conscious personal relationship with Jesus Christ my mind had come alive to thinking; and I became a serious student.

It was recommended that in preparation for seminary training toward becoming a pastor that one should major in the classics—that is, learning Latin and Greek and some of that history. Those who knew "Pip" the professor of Greek in those days at Luther may think me amiss if not mentioning that legendary, compassionate, and dynamic professor. He made us, at least he made me feel through his passionate teaching, that learning Greek was one of the most important things you could ever learn. Occasionally I do use illustrations from Greek to indicate a more precise meaning than it would have in English.

That is clearly true of the four words for "love." In the Greek language, compared to using the same four letter word in English whether talking about loving a car, a house, a game, God or family, in Greek there's a separate word for each of those emphases. Many persons have been exposed to the word "agape" which is the word used in Greek for

God's love–the love of the cross–self-giving and always doing what's best for the other person. Love not based on feelings but concern for the other.

One day while walking down the corridor in the "Old Main" building, my advisor (another caring professor, Dr. Belgum) put his arm over my shoulders and said, "Gary, how's it going?" One part of my response was, "Well, I don't understand why I have to be studying things like Latin and Greek to be a pastor. I just want to preach and teach the Gospel." His response, the truth of which has been reinforced many times was, "Someday you'll understand."

That first year went along very well. While living in the dorm, I had applied to be a dorm counselor. That meant some responsibilities for discipline if things got out of hand on the floor. One may have to say, "Could you please keep that noise down. It's time for people to be asleep." Inspiration to be a dorm counselor may have come from two students the previous semester who had inspired me by their caring and compassionate leadership. Those two upper class men invited all residents who would, to come to their dorm room once a week for Bible Study and conversation, which became a form of counseling. They were clearly interested in strengthening us and in spiritual formation. Prior to that time, I had never experienced such obvious interest in nurturing another person.

During my second year of dormitory living, my roommate was a black man from Southern Rhodesia, Tom Tlou. He was a remarkable scholar and became a campus friend to many. To this day, I can see and hear him as he'd wave his arm to people across campus with whom he had become acquainted. A small majority of whites ruled that country of blacks.

One day on our way to lunch while walking down the dorm corridor, a headline in the paper showed a picture of the incident in which Governor George Wallace of Alabama had sent the dogs to attack a group of black demonstrators. Tom held the paper in front of me and said with some anger in his voice, as he hit the paper with the back of his hand, "Is that the way you treat blacks in this country?" It was either then or later that he had said he could envision himself returning to his home country and promoting violence against the white regime (that would be in response, of course, to the abuse his race had experienced from the white minority in that country).

Tom had gone home with me to meet my parents, and as I recall, my family thought highly of him as a worthy friend. He had graduated from Luther College with high honors. The last we heard of Tom, he had become an ambassador to the United Nations from the Republic of Botswana, Africa.

Paying College Expenses

During that first year of college, as part-time employment, the opportunity presented itself to work for the local tree company. Consequently, I climbed and trimmed most of the trees, at that time, on the Luther College campus. To this day when I walk the campus, I have to check out those trees, especially the one in which by virtue of having my billfold as a buffer, I may have permanently injured my right leg. My foot had slipped off a branch, and I fell down onto the rotating chainsaw blade. My billfold in my back pocket deflected the blade enough to prevent major injury, even though my billfold got nicked by the blade.

Once at seminary in St. Paul, I used that tree trimming experience to work for Kelm Tree Service of St. Paul, Minnesota, as a way to supplement income. Mr. Kelm and I sometimes travelled from job sight to job sight together in his truck. He talked incessantly and often called attention to the many different church denomination signs and wondered why there had to be so many differences if there's truly only one God. A great question for further discussion. However, those questions from a serious businessman remind me of Jesus's prayer for unity in the body of Christ, the Church (John 17).

When we hear today that one obstacle to pursuing higher education is the debt load after graduation, I have some sympathy due to the extra jobs I took on to keep that debt to a minimum, although I know my grades while acceptable for graduation, probably suffered due to time devoted to part-time jobs.

College Year Two Delayed

That summer away from Luther College (between year one and year two) held a surprise I would not have anticipated while working with my father in his dairy business.

While standing in the kitchen of our farm home, I overheard my father say, from his desk in the next room, "If I can't find a man who will work for me for a fair wage, I may have to sell the cheese factory." That comment from my father touched my heart. I've often wondered whether he spoke those words hoping I would hear them.

At this moment, I'm remembering that Dad too had a life plan. He had three sons and now both a farm and cheese factory. He once talked about owning the farm next door to the factory so that more of the milk needed to manufacture cheese could be supplied by his own herds. When cheese was delivered to the Borden Cheese Company warehouse at Marshfield, Wisconsin, it was then tested as to quality. Certain bacteria in the milk could affect the quality of the finished cheese product. A lesser quality could affect the price received by the manufacturer and thus the price Dad could pay the farmers for their milk. At this juncture, it occurs to me how one careless situation on one farm could affect the income all the other farmers would receive. One careless practice on one farm could (due to bad bacteria) lower the quality of that whole vat of milk (nearly ten thousand pounds of milk); and thus, affect the finished product to be sold to the Borden Cheese Company. Consequently, bacteria, invisible to the naked eye, could affect family income for untold numbers of families.

That's also a metaphor of a larger picture of life, behaviors in so many situations can also affect large numbers of people for better or worse. In an off-hand comment one day, I heard my father say that someday perhaps his son would discover a way to detect and remove the bad bacteria that may contaminate the finished cheese product. I remember where he was standing in the factory the day he spoke those words. He was standing near the northeast window of the interior of the factory conversing with a field inspector; I was busy at the vat full of milk about ten yards away. That comment is insight into the very worthy passion and vision he had for his family and business enterprise.

In respect to that farm kitchen comment, I volunteered to work for him one year rather that returning to college for my second year. Some have questioned that decision as a lack of resolve to follow through on a perceived Call into the parish ministry, but that was absolutely not true. I asked my father to allow me to do the work of two employees. That would be my total dedication to save him money and help me build up some financial reserves for college and later seminary. So, that challenge began.

Father and Son in Prayer

One day soon thereafter, Dad and I had a confrontation in the living room of our farm home, the first ever; and we nearly came to blows. Mother as I recall was also in the room sitting down as was I. (As I write this, it occurs to me that they may have planned this moment together. It seems so incredible that Dad and I could ever have had that level of confrontation.) Just in the nick of time before exchange of fists and pushing and shoving might have begun, my father got down on his knees and asked that we pray the Lord's Prayer together. What a moment that was! Dad's spiritual character in powerful demonstration!

At that moment, I think Dad knew my offer to work for him that year had nothing to do with a lack of resolve to pursue becoming a pastor; but I believe he was testing that resolve. (My wife likes to remind me that Dad renewed my cheese maker's license for several years even after I became a pastor, evidently thinking that someday our partnership in that business might continue.

Soon my father began to hire extra help for the summer; and it became clear to me that he would not allow me to do the work of two employees as I had proposed. Once I saw that I was not fulfilling the role I had committed to as one to help him save money as he ran his business, I explained to him again why I had made that decision. So I left home and began working for a salary at Fisher Body Company, and later at the Highway Trailer Company in Janesville, Wisconsin.

As my second year at Luther College began, I also began working as a dishwasher and soon short order cook at Ostrander's Restaurant on Main Street in Decorah. Through the serving window, I could see a high school girl (waitress) whose name was Ella. (She was a member of a refugee family who had arrived at Ellis Island in 1952 from Germany.) She was serving college students and others across the food bar, and sometimes sharing her faith with them. Her poise and faith convictions impressed me.

One evening I held the dustpan for her while she was sweeping the floor. That simple gesture of kindness inspired her to think of me as someone special. A similar emotion inspired me one day while I was eating in the dining room and she walked through the room while waiting on guests. At that moment, I had one of those inspirations that seemed again, a power beyond my comprehension was counseling me to be interested in her as a life partner. Remembering that the Almighty God is all knowing, all powerful, and everywhere present (Psalm 139) I believe now he foresaw the blessed partnership that would unfold into the future we would share together.

As I write this, Ella and I have now experienced fifty-three years of marriage together: three grown children and eight grandchildren. Our marriage ceremony occurred at the South Beef River Lutheran church, my home congregation site, the summer after my graduation from college in 1963. Even though she had a close connection with her Locust, Iowa, congregation, she did not have many extended family in America. As a refugee family, most of her relatives were in Germany. She knew my family, relatives and friends would much more likely attend the wedding in that home congregation of mine than in hers. It was, August 1963 we were married by the elderly Rev. E.B. Christopherson—long time pastor of that congregation. (Occasionally while studying, I notice on the inside cover of a book that it came from his library. His widow years later allowed me to peruse his library and take books of interest to me.)

College, Catfish and Classics!

Among our offerings in that restaurant was a full menu that included sea food. One evening after the local dance hall had closed, the restaurant as usual attracted additional patrons. One group ordered several catfish. Catfish were then deep fat fried and served on platters. Soon one group began returning the catfish because they were frozen in the middle—beautiful on the outside, but frozen in the middle! How embarrassing for this short order cook in the kitchen. Beautiful on the outside, but frozen in the middle! Soon I learned that when the oil in the deep fat fryer has not been changed as frequently as recommended, the finished deep fat product may look beautiful on the outside, golden brown, but not cooked clear through.

Back to the college scene briefly. Since I grew up in a musical family, I decided to try out for the famous Nordic Choir. While trying out for the choir, it was recommended that I take voice lessons instead, and then return for the choir try out. The voice lessons were very helpful, but other priorities kept me from trying out again; however, three years singing in the Messiah Chorus under the direction of

Weston Noble (music conductor with a national and international reputation) have been a lasting blessed memory. Recently on a visit to the Luther College book store, I obtained a copy of a book by Weston Noble and have enjoyed his thoughts in that book. One page in a news magazine a few years ago showed Weston Noble walking the campus picking up trash. What a humble, accomplished, professional.

During the summer of 1959, I was working in the Twin Cities and had to return to return to Decorah to drive school bus for the Decorah School System. Near Chatfield, Minnesota, my car stopped. After rolling it off to the side of the road, I stuck out my thumb to the next driver of the car that came along. That driver stopped and asked where I needed to go. When I told him the Decorah bus barn by 4 p.m., he responded, "I think I can get you there," and he did. Never saw that fellow before or since; but what an incredible commitment by him to a young fellow he'd never met; and so far as he knew may never see again. It just happened to be the next car coming down that road at exactly the right time to help meet my engagement at the bus barn.

More Amazing Grace (Hidden in Trouble)

Later that night I had to hitchhike back to get my car. After no one came along to transport me and after walking all the way to the state line that evening, I decided to hang out at the truck stop that then existed at the intersection north of Decorah, Iowa, home of Luther College. Rather than continuing to walk toward Chatfield, I thought I'd try to catch a ride with a trucker going in that direction. I told my story of my stalled car to a tall, lanky trucker who had just walked in and spread out a map to study. He heard the story and said in response, "I can also go that route to get home, jump in with me, let's go." And I can still remember the roar of that motor between us as he drove the eighteen-wheeler, and I rode along trying to make some intelligent conversation. (Even that voice over engine became significant we learn later in the story). As we got near my stalled

40

car, we ran over a fox. At the top of the next hill, he pulled his large truck off to the side of the road, handed me his flashlight and commanded me, "Go back and get that fox and when I drop you off by your car, you can throw it in the ditch, pick it up tomorrow morning, and collect the bounty."

That moment was another inspirational stroke of Providence that will be picked up in another chapter.

CHAPTER FIVE
Seminary, Internship and First Call
(Truck Driver Epiphany)

"Now to him who by the power at work within us is able to accomplish abundantly far more than all we can ask or imagine, to him be glory in the church and in Christ Jesus to all generations, forever and ever, Amen" (Ephesians 3:20-21).

Almost fifty years later when I walk to the altar to lead worship, I look around at the people present, and I know my Heavenly Father hears as I say to myself, "I'm only a truck driver, a farmer and cheese head person; who am I to be leading these people in worship and proclaiming the precious Word of God to them?" The Holy Spirit is like the wind (John 3) "It blows where it wills" even into the heart of an unsuspecting farm boy. Another example: a best friend all my growing up years was Larry. While driving an eighteen- wheeler truck and listening to Billy Graham on his truck radio, he pulled his truck off to the side of the road; and received Jesus Christ as his Savior and Lord.

As he told the story to me sometime later, he returned home, discarded the liquor and tobacco in his house and began attending worship with his family. It was sheer joy when on a couple occasions he would stop by our home to renew that acquaintance; as we would do when near his home in Janesville, Wisconsin. Conversations and life stories give to our lives much of it's most precious meanings. Larry and his extended family were one of those great life connections for me. In my growing up years they helped me feel significant and that life had purpose and special meaning.

At Larry's funeral, I was asked to serve as a pall-bearer. Bibles were passed on to the family. The Bibles were so well used that they were held together with duct tape. Larry and I had been friends since those earlier days in a one-room country school house. We wrestled under the big trees during recess; not having any idea at the time that wrestling can be a parable of spiritual discernment (Genesis 32:22ff).

My Father had arranged with the school to allow me to come late so that I could pick up one load of milk before school. There was a farmer on another route who spoke scornfully of higher education. He was a tough dude—so to speak. He and his wife had at least ten children. He had a reputation for cruelty to animals. He would occasionally help me load his several cans of milk. During those few minutes, we had some casual visits. His scorn of higher education has always puzzled me, and back then had created a mental hurdle for me to overcome.

Nevertheless, seminary and internship were awe-some and wonderful and have left me with inspiring memories. Among those memories are some businessmen who were also dedicated church leaders in the congregation to which I was assigned for internship.

I also had received great training for pastoral ministry during casual conversations with farmers who helped me consider the expectations of others. One farmer reported to my father that the milk cans and covers were not arranged as he expected. In the administrative language of today, that might be called "attention to detail or quality control."

Morning chapel both at college and at seminary became highlights of the day for me. They gave me a visual of what I someday hoped to be doing, proclaiming and teaching the Word. Many names of college and seminary professors stand out in my mind and have been an ongoing inspiration as I remember some of their messages and spiritual counsel. In particular, I continue to be blessed by a Chapel sermon on the book of Nehemiah, chapter 6, when Nehemiah says to Sanballat, "I am doing a great work and cannot come down. Why should the work stop while I leave it to come down to you?" (Nehemiah 6: 3-4). Sanballat, you may remember, tried with considerable determination to discourage the rebuilding of the city wall after the destruction followed by seventy years of exile into Babylon. Such determination as shown by Nehemiah and follow through are among the ingredients needed for achieving worthwhile goals in ministry for both laity and pastors. Follow through means doing the pastoral work once a Call has been received.

One such moment stands out for me. It was a day when I thought I'd done a full days' work and was very tired. However, the need of a person in an upstairs apartment was on my mind. While not remembering the place, name or details of the visit I do remember being richly rewarded in a spiritual sense for that extra mile effort that day. The achievement I valued was reminding a lonely person that his church was remembering him. That moment has often inspired me to push myself a little beyond what sometimes feels like I've done enough. Living by feelings can be deceiving. Feelings are often like the caboose not the engine that drives the train.

Racial Conflict and Opportunity

Those early seminary days were also the days of the 1960's with lots of stories of racial conflict appeared in the news. (You may recall the story of roommate Tom in a previous chapter.) In the seminary coffee shop/café one could overhear a variety of viewpoints on the racial conflicts dividing America; blacks against whites; conservatives versus liberals viewpoints.

Thankfully, thoughtful people had conceived a program to aid the conversations and create improved insights and understanding. The SIM program (Student Interracial Ministry) program helped create understanding. White seminary students could apply to serve in a black congregation in the South for the summer under the supervision of a black pastor; and black seminary students from the South could apply to serve in a white congregation of the North under the supervision of a white pastor. (Rather than listening to opinions in the seminary café and opinions gleaned from the local news, I wanted firsthand experience with the crises plaguing our country.)

Ella and I made application for (SIM) and were assigned to Parkway Gardens Presbyterian Church in Memphis, Tennessee. We had to go to Charleston, South Carolina, for orientation into that program. Our first-born son, John, just three weeks old, was with us bouncing along in the infant seat even over the Appalachian Mountains and then back to Memphis, Tennessee.

Ella, my dear wife, remembers a phone call from the Seminary President, Dr. Alvin Rogness. He called to report that since we were the only students to apply for the SIM program, they were going to give us the three hundred dollars they had set aside for travel expenses. Rural farm boy as I was, something had created in me a longing for increased understanding of the racial tensions enveloping the consciousness of America at that time.

Rev. Larry Haygood was my supervisor, and I left that year with great respect for him as a pastor and mentor to me. For example, he had no furniture in the living room of his house. That room was left empty as he related to all who would listen and perhaps some who were not listening, to remind him and others of all the black students who needed financial aid to further their education. Some may not have listened because they did not share his depth of passion for such needy students. As long as there was one black student he knew that needed financial aid for education, he would not put furniture in the living room of his house—that empty living room would always be a visual reminder to him of that special need.

His sermon on Psalm 42, one Sunday, also left a lasting impression on me, and I never read that Psalm without thinking of Pastor Larry Haygood and his Sunday sermon: "Hope in God."

Along with the usual pastoral duties, home and hospital visits, and some preaching, I spent many hours that summer studying black history. As I did that, I began to despise my white skin while reviewing all the evil that had been inflicted upon blacks in the South as related by a few of the authors whose accounts I had read: author James Baldwin, among others. Eventually I got over that despising of my white skin which identified me with plantation owners and others who had degraded the black race of people. But I have maintained a passion for reconciliation among the races and have recently received an NAACP membership card.

One day while conducting a dining room devotion, I used the word negro to make a point regarding the first black to be admitted to that college. Two black ladies followed me out of the dining room and chided me for using the word negro. After thanking them for their forthrightness and honesty, I confessed my confusion as to how to refer to them. Their response was so helpful. They said, "Call us blacks, or call us Afro-Americans; or colored; but don't call us negroes. While those comments could have generated some additional discussion, we left the issue with their comments to me.

My internship came that fall after the summer in Memphis. My assignment was to Grace Lutheran in Hilltop Heights, Sioux Falls, South Dakota, under the supervision of Pastor Kenneth Helgeson—another compassionate mentor/leader. Our second son, Timothy, was born during that time, which happened to be the morning of Mother's Day; and I was already assigned to preach the sermon. What a nice Mother's Day memory! Pastor Helgeson and the congregation blessed us in many ways. Then I headed back to seminary for my senior year.

One method of paying bills for us while at seminary was to live in an apartment, which was part of a dormitory for nurses who were getting their training at the Swedish Hospital in Minneapolis. What a great opportunity that was because it meant our rent was paid for by that service of being the caretaker of that large building.

One day while at the seminary, Ella called in panic mode—she had locked herself out of our apartment by leaving the door open for a quick errand down the hall. John, our firstborn, at that time about two years old, had slammed the door shut and; thereby, inadvertently locked himself in, and his mother out.

When I arrived in response to her call, she was sitting on the step in panic mode wondering what harm our two-year-old son was doing inside the apartment. Since, I had an extra set of keys, we went in and found him in the kitchen sitting on the floor. He had opened a container of coconut and was entertaining himself by throwing the coconut up in the air and watching it descend upon himself. We imagined the worst! We knew angels were there in answer to our prayers once again.

One day in a fatherly, grandfatherly manner, President Rogness counseled me on the way from one building to the next. He said, "The fruits of the Holy Spirit include joy and, Gary, you do not always appear joyful."

In retrospect, that brings back a memory from high school days at Lincoln Hill High School in Osseo, Wisconsin. Our geography teacher, tall and kindly Orlando Johnson, said to me one day as I was leaving class, "Gary, you don't smile very much," I must have smiled at him because he added, "there that's better." To this day one rather frequent prayer is, "Lord, let me reflect a joyful heart." Seems I may be quite intensive. Another memory of my father is his saying of me, "Don't tell Gary that wall should be moved, or the next day you may find him moving that wall." To whatever extent such assertiveness may be true, seems it must have come from working with and around dedicated parents.

The day before graduation from seminary with ceremonies to be held in the large downtown Minneapolis Central Lutheran Church building, our first-born son, John, had

had a convulsion; first ever that we had observed. His mother called out in distress with the child in her arms, "Look what's happening!" His hands were flailing and his eyes were rolling. I took him quickly in my arms and rushed to the nearest clinic. Providentially, it seems, that although it was a Saturday, the last person was leaving the clinic building and locking the door at the moment I came running with our child in my arms. She opened the door as I ran toward that clinic with John in my arms. Son John was sent to a local hospital and put on what was thought to be the appropriate medication for his condition.

On Sunday morning before leaving for the graduation ceremonies where families and friends of all graduates would be present, I called the hospital for a report. They responded that he'd had another convulsion which he should not have had on that adult dosage of medication. (We knew he'd had a low-grade fever for several days, which may have helped precipitate the convulsion.)

My reflection on that event, after that morning hospital report coinciding with seminary graduation, was that Almighty God is taking our son to heaven at this time so that I would not forget to proclaim the message of heaven throughout my years of ministry. Even though I'd put that spin on the incident, I did meet Seminary President, Dr. Alvin Rogness as we entered Central Lutheran in downtown Minneapolis, and mentioned to him that I'd appreciate his prayers for our son and added a brief comment on his condition. What a timely encounter that turned out to be!

My intention was that he would remember our son in his private prayers; however, during the prayer part of the graduation ceremony, Dr. Rogness led the whole assembly in prayer mentioning our names and that of our son, John. Incidentally, John has never had another convulsion since that time and has now had a wonderful career as a high school teacher. "Praise God from whom all blessings flow." In the words of Scripture, "He (Almighty God) is able...."

As a first grader, son John's teacher had almost convinced us that he would be a special education student during all of his school years. That teacher, since John was a PK (Pastor's kid), seemed to have unrealistic expectations for him. In the second grade, his teacher was a more grandmotherly kind of person who hugged and nurtured him, and the rest is history. He blossomed as a student under such love and motherly kindness.

As seminary seniors, we were in suspense as to which district (now termed synod) we would be assigned. After being assigned to a synod: east, west, north, south; then will the congregation to call us be rural, small town, or large city. My assignment was to the Northern Minnesota District, and I was given a choice of one of three small town congregations. The Bishop suggested that I could go to either one of the three small towns; but he'd recommend Grygla, Minnesota, because a member of the Call Committee in that congregation was in the dairy business and managed the local creamery. So, there I went in the summer of 1967.

That was a two-point parish, so there were two Sunday morning services: one in town and the other in the country approximately ten miles to the East; and not far from the border of Red Lake Indian Reservation. Wonderful people who again left us with precious memories that have nurtured us through the years. One deacon (Ordean) was among the first to counsel me as he said, "Have you noticed how many more times the Bible says 'come' rather than, 'go'?" I had never thought about that but it was helpful counsel.

That country congregation, Our Savior's Lutheran, were caring, nurturing people and were consistent in their worship attendance and were so very hospitable. As might be expected, remembering them brings back many pleasant memories. One student who lived with her family just down the road from the rural church building made an observation one day that she appreciated that the sermons had a meaningful outline—well organized. Remarkable comment from a high school girl.

Another prominent memory from that small country congregation is of a mother who received her degree from Bemidji State during the time we served that congregation. She and her husband had four boys, high school age and younger. With all that responsibility, she was also pursuing a college degree. Her husband was a farmer and exceptionally faithful at being in that front seat for worship Sunday by Sunday with his arms stretched across the church bench around his sons. He said to me on the way out of worship one Sunday, "Remember, if you see me in the field on Sundays, that I will have also been at worship that morning."

This mother pursuing her degree while raising four children, at one point knew that I was having some difficulty as pastor to the youth group. She gave me some wonderful motherly advice: "Remember, it's your responsibility as pastor to set the boundaries and it's the nature of youth to sometimes rebel, so don't take it personally."

Another of those faithful persons was the man who not only farmed (which included field crops as well as milking cows, raising cattle and hogs), but he also held a second job about fifty miles one way to work a forty-hour a week job in Thief River Falls, Minnesota.

Truck Driver Epiphany Event

One day a forty-dollar check arrived in the mail for the congregation in town, Grace Lutheran Congregation. That check had come from the local bar tender and his wife who ran that facility, which also served as a social center for senior citizens in an attached seating area.

In my mind's eye I can see an elderly woman who lived alone. I'd see her sometimes walking along the street across from my office. Friends and neighbors said of her, "That social center is her only social contact." People who

51

provide and enable such opportunities for real social needs are deserving of our appreciation.

The occasion of a forty-dollar check seemed like a pastoral opportunity to visit and thank the couple. On a Sunday evening, I knocked on the door of their trailer house. That trailer house was located behind the bar facility. She invited me in for coffee and called her husband. He was quite tall, and I recall he had to stoop some to come through that door into the kitchen where we visited over a cup of coffee. He sat in one chair and I sat across the room in another chair. As we visited, I became aware that he was an over-the-road trucker while his wife ran their local business. So, I asked did you ever drive truck in northeast Iowa? "Oh yes," he said and he indicated lots of areas in which he trucked. Then I asked, "Did you ever pick up a person at that truck stop at the intersection north of Decorah, Iowa, and give him a ride to his stalled car, run over a fox and told him to pick it up and turn it in for bounty? He answered, "I thought there was something familiar about your voice!" He was that trucker who had been so kind to me when I was yet a college student approximately five or six years prior to that meeting in their trailer house. What if the bishop, and/or I, had decided on a different one of the three possible northern Minnesota congregations available for me to serve, I would not have been able to make that connection between that ride to my stalled car, running over a fox and that congregation member. Some folks might call that a coincidence; however, to me that was another example of divine intention to encourage call confidence and bless faithfulness in ministry. A fox became another such sign. Other memories surf my mind, too numerous to mention.

One night quite late there was a knock on the door. So, I jumped out of bed and answered the door. The man at the door was drunk and couldn't find his way home. He was about one block away from his home, an apartment building right across from the church building, and I helped him figure that out. Ever since that incident, I've had a fetish to check all the doors at night to make sure they are locked. I can't imagine what might have been our reactions if he had walked right in, stumbled around, walked into our bedroom, or simply sacked out on the floor, how terrifying that could have been.

Another day in the midst of joyful ministry I was being tested to the limit, as to how to handle discipline with a class of around a dozen confirmation students—eighth graders as I recall. After applying every method to class discipline that I thought I'd learned, I finally had to put my books down and march two boys out of class and later reported to their parents. One father called me that night and said, "You won't have any more problems with my son in class." He was correct. That boy was the full back on the football team and in the next classes, after his father's discipline, he (the 8th grader I marched out of class) would tap his finger on the table if any one got a little out of hand and henceforth no more discipline problems with that group.

In that northern Minnesota community, during deer hunting season, people came from miles around to attend an engaging event. Traditionally, we held a 4:30 a.m. worship service for those who both wanted to worship on Sunday and be in the woods early.

One morning as I opened the door to the fellowship hall at about 4 a.m. to continue preparation for that deer hunter's service, I heard movement in the next room. I walked over the wood floor in that fellowship hall stomping my feet as though I weighed 300 pounds. When I flung open the door into the next room there by the kitchen, behind the portable blackboard, I saw two sets of legs. After moving the board, I saw a young man and woman who were shaking in fright. After dismissing her, he and I had a conversation as though I was an authority on such investigations; and we resolved that if he would attend the 4:30 worship service, we'd not pursue the issue any further. And there he was at the service.

That congregation was a combination of four congregations that had come together because of the dwindling numbers in several of the outlying congregations. Appreciation stays in my mind for the pastor who helped to bring realignment to reality—obviously with lots of support by several laity leaders. That in-town building was a combination of three buildings, which had been pulled together to help preserve some identity of former worship connections for those who had given up their geographic building site. That fellowship hall was the former St. Olaf congregational building from up north. The connecting building was the Valle Lutheran Church building—a former congregation to the east. The building was in a horseshoe configuration with the in-town Grace Lutheran building parallel to the St. Olaf fellowship hall across which floor I had stomped to investigate the 4 a.m. noise in the next room. A few people from at least two of the congregations did not join the in-town congregation. Each had identified with another group.

Deer hunting season attracted lots of folks from distant places. After deer hunting hours, a number of hunters would frequent the bars, which were often open after other businesses had closed. One incident of a stranger molesting one of our lovely young member ladies is too personal and possibly still too hurtful to the persons involved. So, we move on.

On to another prominent memory of pastoral ministry in my first pastoral ministry call. After an adult confirmation class, I had the joy of baptizing a young adult who happened to be the local policeman of that small town. We had several conversations about his duties, support, and his reservations as to why he couldn't have certain additional equipment for his duties in such a remote area, forty miles from Roseau, Minnesota; and about that distance from Thief River Falls. Very much a lone law enforcement officer in a small town of around two hundred people, and so distant from other police support; that distance factor seemed to justify his concerns.

At that time, the local mayor was not going to run again because his mother with whom he lived needed more of his time. So, this young man, the policeman, asked if I would run for mayor. That was happening at a time in history when there was some conversation about pastors being more active in civil affairs. Keying off that seminary emphasis, as I thought I remembered it, I said, "I would not seek the position, but if elected I would do my best." That small town of around two hundred people elected me as their mayor. That meant I also became the chief of police. With that added responsibility, every unusual noise especially at night, made me wonder if I'd be called to respond. Only once that I recall was I called to mediate a dispute which actually was settled by the time I arrived at the local bar that night.

All was well until it came time to renew the local liquor license, which of course I had not anticipated when I allowed my name on the ballot for mayor—my error in not becoming better informed. What would our local Pentecostal people, and perhaps some of our own Lutherans think of their pastor signing the liquor license—some could make a mountain out of that issue. Then I remembered that the person who gave me the first tour of that small town, before I had accepted the Letter of Call, had made a major point of telling me that some folks in town felt betrayed when they put the liquor store in because they thought they were voting on whether or not to add hard liquor to their beer license; but it turned out they were really voting on whether to have a state owned or privately owned liquor store. So knowing that, the impression given me was that the majority of the town felt betrayed, *but maybe it was only a few who felt that way;* however, I did some research and found out we could put the issue back on the ballot if we could get the signatures of a certain percentage of those who voted in the last election. I went house to house for those signatures and got the required percentage and then waited for the vote results. In fact, I even went to City Hall and watched the count that night. The vote was overwhelmingly to keep the liquor license. With such a small minority voting against it, I concluded the only persons to vote with me and my wife to reverse the last decision were the Pentecostals.

So rightly or wrongly, I resigned as pastor the next Sunday imagining they didn't think much of their pastor whom they've elected as mayor, and who had been led to believe they would welcome this vote if given the chance. They were now given the chance to dismiss me.

The president of the congregation, a young family man, and a construction worker, came in the next day and asked me to tear up the letter of resignation. At that moment, I felt led to respond that if you want me to continue as your pastor, then you'll have to Call me again with a congregational meeting, which they did.

That president then became quite hostile toward me. He ignored me and would almost spin the tires on his vehicle if he was driving by and I was where I could see him and he could see me.

One day I'd heard that his lovely elementary school daughter had broken her arm while on the school playground. That evening I drove forty miles to the hospital in Thief River Falls to visit his daughter. Her mother was with her at the time. When I returned in the evening from the hospital, I called the father, president of the congregation, who had acted out considerable hostility toward me for resigning as pastor of the congregation. His response to my phone call was "Have you been there already?" "Yes, I replied, I just returned." He responded, "The door is open." And I replied, "Are you inviting me to your house?" He replied, "The coffee's on and there's ice cream in the freezer." So, I went right over and with our visit we probably had a prayer for his daughter's healing. We became friends.

A girl broke her arm. We can read those words without any thought of that girl's physical pain, nor the emotional pain of her parents. That father's hospitality can be interpreted that he was very grateful for his church and the pastor who attended to the concerns he carried in his heart for his daughter. Such are among the joys of being a pastor—a person welcomed into the most precious moments of the lives of the people served. To this day, forty plus years later, I keep the address and phone number of that father near my desk, and we hear from them usually every Christmas.

Delightful and Challenging Surprises

Charlie Wells and his wife lived right next to the church building. Charlie was a self-styled, retired, veterinarian. He was well over six feet tall and his wife Mary was less than five feet. Charlie was blind, so a familiar scene around town was tall Charlie being led around town by his much shorter wife, Mary. When I had the chance to baptize Charlie, he stood up after the laying on of hands and said to me, the young pastor, "Thank you, my son!" Obviously, I still remember that beautiful moment!

Cataract surgery was just becoming more available in those days, and Charlie learned that he may have his eyesight restored at Duluth, Minnesota, even after those many years of blindness. One day I heard the car door slam just outside my office door. There was tall Charlie straightening up after exiting the car—interestingly, I just happened to be in the office at that moment. I greeted and waved to him. He exclaimed, "I can see you." In disbelief, I ran to him and said, "Can you tell me what color my tie is." He told me the color. Still in some disbelief that this man once blind could now see I said, "Can you see the soil conservation office over there?" He exclaimed, "I can see all the way to the creamery." The town rejoiced that their one-time active veterinarian, blind for so many years, could now see. It seemed to some of us like a repeat of the Gospel of John's story of the blind man, "...I was blind now I see" (John 9:25). Soon he was afflicted with cancer and early one morning the pain was such that they called for a time of prayer in their home. His death occurred soon thereafter.

Around that time a tragedy occurred on the farm where my wife's parents lived in northeast Iowa. As mentioned earlier, they were a 1952 refugee family, from Germany to Ellis Island in New York. We have a recent (2015) picture taken of their names on that wall of the Ellis Island wall of names.

Her brother, Gerhard, who was the leader of their rather large farm operation north of Decorah, Iowa, had recently been killed in a farm accident. He had hurriedly sought to remove a faucet from a large barrel to transfer it to another barrel and the torch he was using caused the barrel to explode. He was killed instantly. The theory has been that the barrel from which he tried to remove the faucet had once contained gasoline and thus the reason for the explosion. That barrel was taken to a small town high school as an object lesson for FFA instruction.

Mary, the wife (by now a widow) of the tall Charlie who had received his eye sight after years of blindness, had gone to visit her son in the Quad Cities, Moline, Illinois. We had heard that while there she had been diagnosed with cancer. Though she was a not a member of the congregation, as her husband had been, I felt obligated and honored, to serve as her pastor. Therefore, I called the hospital that morning before worship so I could give the congregation a report; and the nurse at the hospital answered, "If you want to see her alive, you must come soon." So, I announced at the worship service that I would be leaving for the Quad Cities (approximately a five-hundred-mile trip from northern Minnesota to Moline in December weather with a storm in the forecast) immediately after the worship services and if anyone wanted to ride along, please tell me, and I'll pick you up to go along. Two men wanted to go with me because Mary had been like a mother to them.

We literally felt that angels guided us through the storm to her bedside. We planned a stopover at my parent's home. We were stuck once, and I walked to a neighboring farm for a shovel. We were soon on our way to my parent's home. The next morning with the storm still threatening we headed for the hospital to see Mary Wells. When I asked how she'd like me to pray for her, she only wanted me to pray for others whom she named. What a humble and dynamic faith she had! Later after leaving that parish, I was invited back for the funeral.

Since the timing was such, I intentionally drove by the home farm where Ella, my dear wife had lived. It was along the route back to northern Minnesota. Knowing of the recent tragedy of her brother, Gerhard, being killed, it seemed appropriate to check on how things were going on the farm since he had been the farm manager. During a brief conversation, I knew there was frustration at all the work that needed to be done because the main worker and farm manager, Gerhard, was now missing. Because of his death, they were preparing for an auction, to sell out. The father of the family was somewhat handicapped due to an accident while in Romania. Since he was somewhat crippled, Hitler's army did not want him, so he survived that tragic time in the lives of so many Germany people. His brothers were killed in Hitler's army, but due to the rather minor handicap he was able to come with his wife and family to America. Something that looked bad at the time (a broken leg from falling off a horse) became a blessing for the family.

While returning to the parish in northern Minnesota, the Bible verse kept going through my mind, "Bear one another's burdens and so fulfill the law of Christ." Believing I might be the only one who would take the plight of my in-laws to heart to the extent of helping with the farm operation before their planned auction, I felt called to resign my Call in northern Minnesota and help them on the farm until they had had their auction. After all I grew up in the dairy business and felt I could do what needed to be done. (An auction will provide better returns if cattle and surroundings appear in good health and repair.) In support of that decision was also the fact that Ella had been frost bitten as a child, and the cold weather of that northern country was an added trial for her. Her doctor had recommended moving farther south away from those cold Minnesota temperatures. Again, doing what I thought the Lord was counseling me to do I simply trusted the Lord for my future knowing that assistance on the farm would be temporary; and we insisted that it be without financial remuneration, except for living in the one vacant house on the other farm. That move was made in northern Minnesota January weather, even though I'd been warned through the District Bishop's Office that with that decision to resign, I might never get back into the ministry. After the auction on my in-law's farm and our few weeks of assistance, I called the district president of the Iowa District and he had me in an Iowa parish, Rolfe, Iowa, the next Sunday. Once again, I was inspired to trust the guidance of the Holy Spirit, whose workshop is the Holy Bible. "He is able..." and "Bear one another's burdens and in this way you will fulfill the law of Christ" (Galatians 6:2).

In the words of Thomas Keating and his book *Open Heart, Open Mind*, "Nothing can stand still on the spiritual journey" (P. 7).

CHAPTER SIX
Families, Motorcycle, Poetry and Mourning

"I can do all things through him who strengthens me"
(Philippians 4:13).

Why was there a pastoral vacancy at this time at St. Paul's Lutheran of Rolfe, Iowa? A part of the answer is that the person troubling the former pastor, supposedly, had been "dethroned." Guess who was my tour guide when I arrived for a first tour? It was he. Thankfully by now the Board had grown a bit wiser and informed him, "We have our authorized teaching materials and your private theology we do not authorize." Soon that young, passionate fellow (with whom I enjoyed several visits) found a new site in which to express his faith. Pastors are greatly aided in ministry when elected leadership make such caring decisions in the interest of truth and unity.

Rolfe is located in Pocahontas County, Iowa. A roadside statue of Pocahontas, the Indian Princess, who married John Rolfe, is located on the north side of the highway as you enter the town of Pocahontas, approximately twelve miles southwest of Rolfe. Those names provide an interesting historical reflection on the naming of those two towns. Why would two mid-western towns be named after an Indian Princess (perhaps the most famous Indian Princess), and her husband, whose historical roots were so far to the

East? (It's a question needing further investigation and I long to know that answer.)

Incidentally, Rolfe is also the town in which one former president of the University of Iowa was born and raised, President Hancher, also a Rhodes Scholar. One other celebrity name associated with the Rolfe community, a treasured memory of one restaurant manager, is the name of the once popular dance band leader, Laurence Welk, who had one day entered her restaurant for a meal. She liked to remember that special day and that special guest.

Five years of ministry among those Rolfe, Iowa, people once again brought into our lives beautiful memories of dedicated, caring and nurturing people. (Some congregations seem to me to be like specialty centers for nurturing young pastors). This was another of those places. Our children began their elementary school journey in Rolfe and graduated from high school in the next parish to which we were assigned. We have a picture of our oldest son, John, peddling a bicycle—mounted ice cream freezer ringing his bell and going street to street—a precious memory of those days and the nurturing of a young family. Timothy, our second oldest was frightened by a neighbor boy. One day he announced gleefully that he was no longer afraid of that boy. He said I thought of David and Goliath and my fear went away.

While in Rolfe, we also experienced the need to sell the family dog, a St. Bernard. Enterprising Ella had wanted to raise and sell St. Bernard puppies, but our St. Bernard never bore pups. However, our three children had become very attached to Faithful (the dog's name). So, it was quite traumatic for them once we announced that we'd found a new home for Faithful. When the decision was announced at the kitchen table one evening, our three children all put their eating utensils down simultaneously, and one exclaimed, "You didn't sell Faithful did you?" We had some explaining to do.

Due to the much waste feces material and the loud bark, we needed to disengage with the large dog Faithful, and perhaps obtain a smaller, quieter dog for the children. Soon we owned a small white poodle we named Frosty. The name fit the dog's color.

One day it seemed appropriate to visit a family who had recently moved into the community right across the street from the parsonage and the beautiful church building. As I knocked on the door of that house, I was met by the housewife who was wearing a sweatshirt with the bold letters "Go to Hell." We had a brief visit, and I invited them to worship with us. They were soon persons who attended worship regularly. The last I heard, this woman and her husband were custodians of that church building. Another reminder, "Don't judge a book by its cover." "Go to Hell" could have been the basis for some discussion, but at that time it seemed prudent to ignore those three words and choose the alternative route, "Please come to worship."

Ella, my dear and wonderful wife, became the youth group choir director. The choir loft in which the choir rehearsed was directly across from the pastor's office. It was a beautiful day and the window to that office was open toward the South with a clear view of the street. When youth group choir rehearsal was over on this particular day, Ella came into my office, a bit exhausted and frustrated because discipline measures were needed to get through the youth choir rehearsal. She expressed the thought, something like, "Some days I wonder if it's really worth it."

At that very moment, we heard a voice on the street that passes that church building. That voice was the voice of one choir member, one of the more difficult persons to keep focused during the choir practice. Now he was standing on his pedals, pedaling his bicycle down the street at a fast pace. We could see him through the open window, and he was singing at the top of his voice the very song they had rehearsed in choir "Everybody ought to know who Jesus is!" Ella and I looked at each other there in the pastor's office and said something like, "I guess it's really worth the effort after all." That boy was (is) the son of the woman who had met me at the door with those bold letters on her pull-over shirt.

One wonderful tradition in that place was the adult Sunday School class held after the worship service. One Sunday, as class began after I had been gone on vacation, there was an issue the group wanted to discuss. The pastor who had filled in for me the Sunday before had used a rather dramatic illustration to make a point. He threw a Bible on the floor, so I was told, and exclaimed, "It's just paper and ink." There were differing interpretations of the meaning of that dramatic illustration. On the one side was what they interpreted as disrespect shown to the Bible. Another interpretation was that those words in ink on the paper, called the Bible, need to be read, received, and hidden in the heart before they become empowering for Christian living (Colossians 3:16; Psalm 119:11 & 105); otherwise, without that reception in the heart of a person, that pastor supposedly was trying to illustrate that the book is just filled with ink and paper. That was a dynamic committed group of people— some of their testimonies continue to warm my heart. What a joy it was to share the precious Word of God with such dedicated Christian people. Wonderful they were! Interestingly, two of the very faithful men in that group were on totally opposite sides of the political spectrum. One was as committed to a conservative philosophy as the other was to a more liberal political democratic point of view. How wonderful that they could Sunday after Sunday share in that hour of Bible Study and discussion. One day one of the two men said to me, in private, if that man doesn't stop sharing his political views in Bible class there's going to be trouble. To the best of my ability, I tried to steer the class discussion away from political issues.

Those were also the days when the gas prices went very high. That created a dilemma for individuals and congregations. For some congregations there was not an immediate connection made between car allowance and that added expense for pastors making their pastoral calls. In that parish, hospital calls sometimes had to be made all the way to an Iowa City hospital; sometimes to Rochester, and that added considerable travel expense. One solution, the one I chose, was to buy a motorcycle at Emmetsburg, Iowa, for better gas mileage. Since it was a Suzuki 350, the semi-trucks passing me on the freeways created enough draft to almost sway the cycle and rider. A constantly repeated prayer during many of those cycle rides was, "Lord save me for your continued Kingdom Service." Soon I traded for a 500 Suzuki—a little larger cycle. Occasionally I'd come home either rain soaked or very chilled. My dear wife would comfort me by wrapping herself around me to warm my body with hers.

A young man in that congregation had gotten himself involved in a cult while away to a southern state for college, and that created a burdened soul for his faithful Christian parents. He had also recently purchased a Subaru vehicle, which was getting him as much as thirty miles to the gallon of gasoline. That gave me a good reason to sell the motorcycle (after riding it twelve thousand miles), and buy a Subaru car that could get near the same mileage as the motorcycle. It really felt good to have a roof over my head again while traveling and doing normal pastoral calling, especially on those rainy and chilly days.

One night there was a knock on the door. (Enterprising Ella was gone to market candles she had made to supplement the family budget.) The person at the door exclaimed with a big smile, "I've been baptized." That was the fellow who had inspired me to buy a Subaru car, who had also gotten himself into a cult, burned incense to an image in his bedroom above the family kitchen, and as mentioned, that greatly burdened his faithful Christian parents. After that trauma had weighed on the family for some time, an Evangelical couple, relatives, invited the young man to live with them in Fort Dodge, Iowa, on the condition that he would attend worship at their church with them. (Obviously, there must have been some counseling by that family, too, which led him to be baptized as an adult.)

In the newspapers, a few months after his baptism, there had been a story of a religious group butchering chickens near, or on the City Square in Fort Dodge as part of a religious ritual related to Satan worship. This fellow who had just knocked on the door and who said, "I've been baptized" needed to talk about his possible role, at least in his imagination, in attracting these Satan worshippers to that city. We had conversation—confession and absolution.

That young man, now a confessing Christian, began to write poetry. His once so burdened mother (the husband and father was less expressive) now rejoiced and spoke on how blessed she felt that her son was now writing such beautiful words expressing his new-found faith in Jesus. He was a new creation, the old had passed away (11 Corinthians 5:17) and the new had come into his life.

One day the local papers would probably have headlined the story of a young man found face down, drowned in the river near Bradgate, Iowa. Someone riding a bicycle across that bridge saw a body face down in the river. No one, to my knowledge, ever knew why this young man, who recently had become an Evangelical Christian and had been writing Christian poetry, was wading the river that day; and secondly why he had drowned in the rather shallow water. One theory was that he may have been trying to withdraw from some chemicals to which he may have become addicted and in that state of mind had a physical reaction that caused him to fall face down into the water and drown. That's only one theory, and I had never heard any other explanation.

That was one of the largest funerals I had ever conducted. In a follow-up conversation with the parents two things vividly stand out in my memory: 1) The father confessed, yes, we always took our children to church, Sunday School, Confirmation, and did those expected things; but we didn't talk much about our personal faith in our home and what Jesus really means to us. *What a Lesson for all parents!* Help your children and grandchildren understand how to apply the teachings of the Bible and faith to everyday life situations by talking about that with them. *More important today than ever, don't leave that important application of the meaning of a personal relationship to Jesus Christ to others. Help your children know what that means to you and how it affects your daily decisions and living.* 2) Those parents also volunteered these words of permission and counsel to me, "Pastor, you have our permission to tell our story to whomever may be helped by it." Now that story has been told one more time.

One day three men from Moville, Iowa, were with us for Sunday morning worship checking me out to see whether they'd like to call me to be their pastor at Trinity Lutheran of Moville. (I had indicated to the Bishop that after five years in Rolfe, I was ready for another Call.) Ella invited the three men for dinner at the parsonage, right after the worship service and Sunday School. Three tall, strong men hung their heads in that parsonage dining doom and one of them said, "If we'd have known how much he (our pastor) was hurting, we would not have put the kind of pressure on him that we did." (*Another reminder, we don't know how much we don't know—so let's learn from one another ASAP.*)

Soon after five and one half years at the Rolfe congregation, we were settled at Moville, Iowa, and I had resigned as dean of the Fort Dodge Conference to make this move. In this new setting the parsonage was right across from Woodbury Central School. The parsonage is also the first house south of the church building. Geographically, we made a change; but many precious memories linger from those years at Rolfe, Iowa.

CHAPTER SEVEN
Hope and Recovery, Boat People Hospitality

*"And the King will answer them, 'I assure you: whatever you
did for one of the least of these brothers of mine,
you did for me'»* (Matthew 25:40).

Our next venture in marriage and ministry became
a training center for reconciliation ministry. While
at this particular parish ministry setting, a local
counselor and hospital chaplain, Rudy, paid me a wonderful
compliment that reminds me of the words attributed to
Mark Twain, something like, "I can live for ... so many days
on one good compliment." This chaplain/counselor said, "I
don't know of anyone who could have brought such healing
to that congregation."

That compliment completely amazed me. It hadn't
seemed like that much of a challenge, but it brought back to
mind a bit of advice that had guided me, focus on Christ, and
the rest will take care of itself. One Sunday morning my
heart soared with joy as I saw two faithful Christian men
who had had differences on how to support their former
pastor now conversing across from one another at the same
table during adult Sunday School fellowship.

One point of view on how to support that former pastor was to support, affirm, and counsel. Another point of
view was: we need different leadership because we've got a
special group of youth who need a different style of ministry.

Due to having three children in the school system, I evidently seemed to fit what they thought they needed in pastoral leadership.

That former pastor, a Korean War veteran, was seemingly suffering the Post Traumatic Stress Syndrome before that was recognized and formal treatment offered as it is today. His attempted suicide by hanging himself in the church basement was unsuccessful due, in part, to the intuitive feelings of his wife who came running to the church, saw him in that condition, and then went screaming outside to a group of people on a neighboring lawn, who were also members of that congregation, and then helped rescue him. Thankfully, through that pastor's son, also now a pastor, we learned that after treatment first at a Sioux City Hospital, and then at a Chicago facility, that pastor became the happiest that his son could ever remember. (Thanks to his conscientious wife, the rescuing congregational members, efficient medics and others, that pastor who sought to harm himself got rushed to appropriate aid and treatment.) Much gratitude to those who assisted in the rescue of that dear man in his time of very special need.

One morning it was evident that the church building of this parish had been broken into and money collected for World Hunger had been stolen. Within a few days in the news, we heard that someone had been caught breaking into a church in South Sioux City, Iowa; and that person was now in the Woodbury County Jail.

Curiosity made me wonder what kind of person would break into a church and do the things reported about this person. With a goal of hoping I could help him turn his life over to the Lord Jesus by reminding him that the money he'd stolen had been gathered for World Hunger, I thought that might be convicting to him, but don't recall as I visited him in the jail that it made much impact.

One benefit of that call to the jail was to be reminded by one of the officers that there was no one doing chaplaincy work at the jail at that time, and he wondered whether I'd be interested. As it turned out I was, and did that for the next eight to nine years. Gideon's International provided Bibles for me to distribute to inmates and that gave me some good conversation opportunities with them. Thankfully, the congregational Board affirmed and supported that extension of their ministry.

During that time, there was also a change in jail administration. In my mind, this was a very instructive and dramatic learning experience. With the new administration, rather than seeing and overhearing bold, almost bragging conversations on roughness with the prisoners being admitted, there was a significant change in mood and atmosphere from loud shouting to quiet and no more scenes and conversations with seemingly gleeful tones on the issue of treating prisoners roughly. This was an excellent illustration of the power of effective management and supervision. Much more could be said on why and how wise leadership goals can protect and help heal and sustain already troubled, hurting souls and their families. Coincidentally, at this time (fall 2016), there has been a series of articles in the Waterloo Courier, daily newspaper on mental illness. One of those articles featured the headline: "Jails a last resort for treating mental illness."

Well into those ten plus years of ministry in the Moville Parish, the phone rang with the message given that a boy was missing and his family had searched and was unable to find him. We were probably asked to remember them in prayer, but driving out to the farm of this very loving and humorous family seemed also an appropriate response. When arrived, we saw emergency vehicles parked along the roadside.

Near the time all hope of finding that kind, handsome teenage boy (with some mental/emotional dysfunction) was fading, someone decided, to check an abandoned house just up the hill a few rods. We walked through the house, upstairs and downstairs, checking every possible hiding place with no success. As we were leaving the house, one of the Emergency Responders suggested looking beneath the kitchen floor boards. There were a few loose boards in the kitchen of that abandoned house. That Emergency Responder, got down on his belly and peaked beneath those floor boards with his flashlight and there was the boy—over in a corner, trembling with fear, hugging his dog. That young fellow had been walking his dog around the farm pond on the far end of the farm while his parents thought he was missing. Upon return from the walk, he saw the emergency vehicles and in panic, we think, took refuge in that house. A happy ending—thanks to the Emergency Responder who followed his intuition to check beneath those kitchen floor boards. How that boy got beneath those loose boards seems a testimony to the panic mode that had overtaken him.

Private Pilot

Our home in that community was five miles east of a grass air strip I passed every time I traveled into Sioux City. An ad appeared in the paper stating that for five dollars one could fly with a pilot to explore one's interest in becoming a private pilot. My years on board the USS Philippine Sea CVS 47 Aircraft Carrier in the Pacific Ocean, watching those propeller-driven planes take off and land, perhaps piqued my interest in flying. So, I took that five-dollar flight opportunity and began training to become a private pilot. Some cope with life's stresses by taking time to golf, to go fishing, and to watch TV. At this point in my life, I chose as my diversion to become a private pilot.

My final test, after approximately forty hours of training, was delayed by my flight instructor because I had trouble landing that small plane in a cross wind. However, I was at the point that I could take the plane up by myself from the airport at Le Mars, Iowa, without the flight instructor with me. Knowing that cross-wind landings were my obstacle for the final flight test and getting a license, I chose one somewhat windy day thinking that if I'm ever going to master this skill I'd better stick with it. It was a borderline windy day when one might have decided, better not fly to-day; but I did. When I came in for a landing with a fairly strong cross wind, my flight instructor happened to have ar-rived. Knowing I was out in that wind he was standing by the runway as I came in for the cross-wind landing. And, knowing my lack of expertise landing in a cross wind, I won-dered whether he was thinking he'd be watching a plane wreck. Once on the ground he said, "If you can do that, you are ready for your test flight," which then soon happened at the Sheldon, Iowa, airport. I had my private pilot license, which I continue to carry in my billfold.

One experience of my approximately two-hundred-fifty hours of flying slightly terrifies me when I remember it. Grandma Hoff had died, and we planned to go to the fu-neral. Thinking at that time, flying together as a family in that rented plane with me as pilot seemed appropriate. This was an unforgettable experience in unforeseen circum-stances. My parents planned to meet us at the airport in Winona, Minnesota. All was well until time to land. There was cloud cover, and we could not see the airport. If one is qualified appropriately as an instrument rated pilot with ra-dar skills, that would not be a problem. However, with no such instrument rating, I was really getting nervous with the family in the plane. I thought, "How do we land if the airstrip is cloud covered?" While in an internal panic mode—not aware the family shared my anxiety at that moment, son John (about 11 years old at that time) said, "Dad, there's a hole in the clouds." Pilot Gary, aimed the plane for that hole in the clouds, that separation in the cloud cover. WOW! There was the airport landing strip at just the right angle for a safe landing.

Once again, it seemed the Almighty knew our plight, and in His omnipotence and omniscience provided the res-cue plan by that separation in the clouds and our young son's intuition/inspiration to call attention to it. Of course, I was grateful not to be further embarrassed by having a plane mishap in front of my parents, say nothing of the pain it may have caused them; and possible injury to the family and damage to the rented aircraft.

On a more positive note, Mother a few years later became a nursing home patient at the care center at Osseo, Wisconsin. Knowing my father's favorite musical sound was the violin, I took a few lessons and with that private pilot ability to decrease travel time, I made a few trips by plane to that nursing care center to visit and play a few hymns on the violin for my mother. Hopefully, those were consoling times for her.

Pastors also have the challenges as do all parents, of raising and training their children. Timothy (our second oldest) brought home reports of being challenged and picked on by another student. (One has to take driver's training to drive a car, but for being parents you're just winging it with whatever good counsel one might pick up along the way.) In the case of son Tim's conflict with another student, I purchased a set of sixteen-ounce boxing gloves— pretty puffy—couldn't really hurt anyone with them unless you're a real big powerhouse. I recommended that he invite his friend to the house and challenge him to a boxing match. One afternoon I came into the house and noticed the light was on in the family room downstairs. There were the two, previously at odds, now each on opposite sides of a make-shift boxing ring, both sweating, and both smiling as though best friends. Guess it worked—don't recall that problem between the two ever emerged again.

About this time, hoping visual exposure to famous historical sights might assist our children's learning experiences in school, it seemed prudent to take a trip to some of those historic sights of our country. We rented a motor home out of Galesville, Wisconsin, and included my parents and a bachelor uncle on that long trip: Niagara Falls, United Nations in New York, Washington D.C., Disney World, and eventually back home. It was a memorable, safe and rewarding trip. To this day, we hear an occasional reference to that trip.

Another day while serving in this Moville parish a shocking phone call arrived that a nephew, Todd, had been killed in a traffic accident just outside Osseo. His vehicle had been rear ended while waiting to turn toward the home of the girl he would soon marry. Todd was a dear cousin admired by our children. We called the children home and soon we were all on our knees on the kitchen floor in prayer together. Such are moments of blending ministry to many others with ministry to one's own family.

Ella reminds me that about this time I went back to Osseo to visit my father in the hospital. While at his bedside, I utilized a learning from the Evangelism Explosion teaching questions, "Dad we trust you'll be getting well soon, but when you die, do you feel that you will go to heaven?" My father's response with hands across his chest blessed me as he said, "Nothing in my hands I bring, simply to thy cross I cling." He had an eighth-grade education and had been a hard-working farmer with callouses on his hands as proof. There were no Christian education programs going on at the time, but his faith was nurtured through Sunday by Sunday worship hearing the Word and singing the hymns. One couldn't ask, it seems to me, for a better assurance that Dad was ready to continue his earthly journey; and, also, ready to depart for his heavenly dwelling.

Around this time, during a family conversation, Dad caused a moment of suspense and silence after we heard him say, "I saw the angels once." It was not his character to speak of his faith in that way. So, I said, "Dad, when did you see the angels?"

One day he was driving into the neighboring farm driveway when he had feelings causing him to turn around, go home and tell his wife (my mother) to call the ambulance. He'd had a heart attack.

The hospital staff in charge, within a day or two, said that he was ready to go home. About that time, he had another attack so severe they had to bring him back to life with shock treatment. It was then, as Dad explained, that he had seen the angels.

Youth ministry was a highlight of those years at Trinity Lutheran in Moville. As a dad, I had the privilege of guiding the three of our own children through those years in Confirmation and youth groups. That included a couple of trips to National Youth Gatherings, which were always a wonderful inspiration. A great part of that inspiration was the awareness that all those youth, usually twenty to thirty thousand of them, were gathered together for that inspiration. Such gatherings help them to know the church is an awesome body of Believers—larger than any single congregational youth group. Tony Compolo continues to be a speaker in demand for such occasions. At one of those Youth Gatherings I learned another important lesson, "Pay attention to where you are standing." While waiting with a few others for transportation to arrive I felt some discomfort on my legs. Soon one of the group nearby exclaimed, "You are standing on a red ant hill." By that time the pain was so intense I ran to a restroom where I could rid myself of those biting little creatures.

Family devotional times around the kitchen table are precious to remember. *Pilgrim's Progress* and another book of Bible stories were among our many readings during those years along with the Bible and other devotional books. On one occasion, I had mentioned the word "divorce" in reference to something, the details of which I do not remember. Maybe it was a newspaper article, or perhaps something related to one of our devotional readings. What I do remember, quite vividly, was the look on our children's faces when the word "divorce" was mentioned. At that moment—due to those facial expressions and children gazing at one another—I resolved that word would never be heard again from me in front of our children.

While I know, some marriages need to end due to traumatic dysfunction, many could be saved if both partners were humble enough to seek counsel through a qualified counselor.

Thankfully, now after fifty plus years of marriage, divorce has never been a discussion concerning our marriage; but I can't forget the look on our children's faces when that "d" word was mentioned around our table in their presence. Seems they might have overheard comments and sensed some emotional pain in the lives of others that they didn't want to become a part of their family experience.

Midway through our years at the Moville parish I'd been wrestling with some abdominal pains doctors were having difficulty diagnosing. They suspected it could be gall bladder. The pain became so intense that I asked Ella, my dear wife, to rush me to the hospital.

Recovery required some down time during which I painted the following words on a slab of wood which continues to stand in the stairwell of the house we now live in forty years later. At times, I've found some comfort in reviewing this message "IF" by Rudyard Kipling.

If you can keep your head
When all about you are losing theirs and blaming it
on you,
If you can trust yourself, when all men doubt you,
But make allowance for their doubting too.
IF you can wait and not be tired by waiting, or
being lied about
Don't deal in lies,
or being hated, don't give way to hating,
And yet don't look too good, or talk too wise;
If you can dream and not make dreams your
master;
If you can think and not make thoughts your aim;
If you can meet with triumph and disaster,
And treat those two imposters just the same;
If you can bear to hear the truth you've spoken
Twisted by knaves to make a trap for fools,
Or watch the things you gave your life to broken,
and stoop and build them up again with worn out tools;

If you can make one heap of all your winnings
and risk it on one turn of pitch and toss, And lose at
start again at your beginnings And never breathe a word
about your loss;
If you can force your heart and nerve and sinew
To serve your turn long after they are gone;
And so hold on when there is nothing in you
Except the will which says to them "Hold on."
If you can talk with crowds and keep your virtue,
Or talk with Kings—nor lose the common touch;
If neither foes not loving friends can hurt you; If all
men count with you but none too much;
If you can fill the unforgiving minute with sixty
seconds worth of distant run- Yours is the Earth
and everything that's in it;
And which is more—you'll be a man My Son!

Aid to Immigrants

Those years in the community of Moville were also the
years of boat people fleeing from Vietnam. The congregation, Trinity Lutheran, in Moville sponsored two families
who lived with us in the basement of the parsonage while
getting acclimated with driver's license, Social Security
cards and other necessities. The older man, Vi, was a businessman who continued his expertise in Sioux City. His
wife, Lam, recently sent us an e-mail (September 2016) telling us that she had just come upon the newspaper article in
which it was reported that she had been robbed at gunpoint
by one of her employees.

The young couple went to work at IBP and faithfully
worked there and prospered. Yes, they prospered! Soon they
were living in a nice house in South Sioux City. They also
owned a nice vehicle and they had a large screen TV. Rumors began that as immigrants they did not have the same
payroll deductions that American citizens do. Curious about
such rumors, I asked to see one of their check stubs and noticed they have the same deductions as everyone else working at IBP. Muoi said one reason they appear to be doing so

well financially is that when he is asked to work overtime, he does. American men often say, when asked to work overtime that they must go fishing; or take their wife dancing. Muoi said since he doesn't fish nor dance he can work overtime when asked.

One day when the phone rang, it was the sister of Muoi (the IBP employee who worked there with his lovely wife, Thieu). Muoi's sister was calling from Florida. Muoi had been frightened at his place of employment and felt that the communists were pestering him in America even after thinking he had fled from them as he left Vietnam. His sister wanted me to know and, if necessary, please help him arrange to go to Florida to be near her.

(A little background here may be helpful). During the days of assisting Muoi with drivers training, license, etc., we developed a routine that whenever he wanted to help me pay for something, for example gas for our trips taking him to work, I would say, "Jesus helps me, so I help you." Since I knew that he and his family were starting over in America and had very limited material assets, I was glad to help. Now that he was so frightened by what he thought were communists stalking him, I went to his trailer house to visit with him (in response to his sister's call) and tried to convince him that the incident that frightened him had nothing to do with the communists. I was told someone had bumped his chair in the cafeteria and he fell. Finally, having no success to talk him out of wanting to move to Florida near his sister, I fell back on our routine of saying, "Jesus helps me and I help you." So, before leaving for the night and feeling that seemingly he was resolved to move to Florida, I concluded the conversation with, "Muoi, Jesus helped you out of Vietnam, Jesus helped you to Malaysia and to California and to Iowa, and to get a job. Jesus will help you now, too." There was a pause and then he responded, "Thank you, Father." (He routinely called me Father). That settled him and he remains living in South Sioux City and working at IBP, unless by now he may have retired. Another story of "the name of Jesus calms our fears."

In the fall of 2015, a Facebook message was received from a member of the other Vietnamese family who had by now settled in California. He (Huy—two years old when he arrived in America, now thirty-seven) wondered whether we were the ones who helped them settle in America. The answer to that question was "yes," but it needs to be recognized that wouldn't have happened without congregational support and approval.

Huy said that he had become Christian but his parents (Vi, the businessman, and his wife) had not, could we come out and see them. We flew out and among our activities with them, we attended the Mariners Church Worship Service. While there after the service we were thanked by several members of that congregation for assisting those Vietnamese, especially Huy, to come to America. He serves on the board of that large congregation, which facilities occupy fifty acres in Irvine, California, and he provides so much good leadership they wanted to thank us for helping them come to America.

Occasionally while walking from the parsonage in Moville to the church office, I considered that it was time, after ten plus years, for someone else to have the opportunities we had had in that parish setting. Ella had graduated from Morningside College located in Sioux City during our years at Moville. (She jokes that it took her seventeen years to get through college because she'd pick up a few courses in each parish we served, beginning at Thief River Falls, Minnesota in the late 1960s.) At the time of her graduation, I wondered how a major in business administration and a minor in art would complement our journey together. Long story short, many times I've been thankful for what has become a beautiful set of skills for our ongoing marriage and journey together.

Further, our children had received wonderful music training at Morningside College on the piano, violin and cello. Our daughter Gretchen had graduated at the head of her class, Valedictorian and sang to her class as part of her Valedictorian Address: "I could wish you money....but when I've wished you Jesus, I've wished you everything." She was applauded by that gathered graduation assembly. And this was (is) a public school. She boldly proclaimed a conviction that seemed to have possessed her.

We left that parish, with a wonderful farewell. What a joy to see those persons taking time to come together simply to bless this pastor and family on their way to their next adventure in ministry. What a blessing to remember that farewell gathering. "Blest be the tie that binds, our hearts in Christian love," a song inspired by a similar occasion in the life of that author/pastor.

CHAPER EIGHT
Recommended and Rejected

"Trust in the Lord with all your heart, and do not rely on your own insight. In all your ways acknowledge him, and he will make straight your paths" (Proverbs 3:5-6).

At the end of approximately two years in this next Call, there was a vote on whether or not I should continue as their pastor. That Palm Sunday vote (1988) remains etched in my mind. While difficult for the family, that memory remains for me a source of joy and strength—a serene sense of the Holy Spirit's counseling—preparing—and guiding.

One morning, Ella, my dear and faithful wife, was standing by the mirror in our bedroom preparing herself for the day. I had just awakened from a special dream; a dream of a craftsman polishing stones. So real and powerful was that dream that I had to tell her about it immediately upon awaking. That became a parable of life for me in that parish. A prominent leader in that community was heard to say, "Olson doesn't fit well in this community," and I'm quite aware of who precipitated that commen, and the reason he made that statement. Soon I was without a Call and took on a couple of temporary jobs to earn dollars to pay living expenses.

In the midst of such vocational ventures, one family incident remains fixed in my mind. Upon arrival home one day to that parsonage, I saw a motorcycle helmet laying on the kitchen counter. That was our elder son's way of introducing us to the fact that he'd become a motorcycle enthusiast. He and his wife eventually would take a trip to the West Coast on a motorcycle. One evening on the trip they were offered the hospitality of staying overnight in a motorcycle dealership. Once when discussing how he could have become so interested in motorcycles, I was reminded by another family member that they used ride behind me on my motorcycle as I drove them to Bible Camp.

Incidentally, one of the elders in the Rolfe congregation, at which time I'd purchased a motorcycle, had made a luggage device for my cycle with the form of a cross at the top. That kind and memorable gesture and luggage device made those trips with children safer as they rode behind me to Bible Camp. Those Bible Camp experiences had also brought our elder son into relationship with a family who owned property around the Okoboji Lakes area. That relationship has resulted in son, John, becoming a real estate investor in the area along with his vocation as a teacher; and has now involved us, his parents, in that real estate interest, too. Rich family blessings around that lakes area all started with trips to the Bible Camp located near one of those lakes.

After that digression into family experiences, we come back to the parish we were serving at the time we were introduced to the motorcycle stories.

Perhaps no one knows the range of issues foisted upon whomever would have received that Call to serve Bethesda Lutheran congregation, following a dearly loved long term pastor's pastorate. A few of those issues will become more obvious in the paragraphs that follow.

In recent years, the wisdom of years and experience has dictated a longer term pastorate may require a longer period of time with a temporary call pastor—usually termed an interim ministry. There are pastors who specialize in that type of ministry.

That former pastor had a reputation as a kind Evangelical leader. His name and that of his sons, I remember hearing mentioned with great respect and reverence.

The church occasionally introduces a new hymnal. Bethesda Lutheran had chosen to bypass a couple of the latest editions. Every congregation has that option. That also may create tension in relationships if a new pastor believes that adapting to the new hymnal would be faithful to the scriptures and appropriate.

In retrospect, that Call, urged upon me by the Bishop, became a two-year holding pattern for our next Call to Bethel Lutheran congregation of Parkersburg, Iowa. (Look for that story in the next chapter.)

Holding pattern is my interpretation of why I was called to that Bethesda Parish in Jewell, Iowa, with a sign reading as you enter the town "A Gem in a Friendly Setting." Recently while sorting through some files, I came upon the letter from a Synod staff member commending me to that Call with the statement that the Synod staff thought I'd be a good match for that parish. One pastor who interviewed before me for that Call, had said, "You may not have that new hymn book the first week I'm here as your pastor, but you would have it the second week." Obviously, he was not called. Whether to have the latest edition of the hymn book was one of several issues facing that congregation at that time. By the time I arrived, that new hymn book was in boxes yet to be opened and placed in the worship center. One group of ladies asked me on one occasion how I would feel if several of them stood up and walked out of the service in protest against the new hymnal.

Our second son, Timothy, visited us at Jewell and also visited the barber shop for a haircut. He had finished a term of youth ministry with Peace Lutheran, Burnsville, a suburb of Minneapolis, Minnesota. He'd had some thoughts of going on to seminary, but during his brief time in the barber shop and with the stresses he sensed at this time in the Jewell parish, he decided pastoral ministry was not for him. Probably he'd had other thoughts too as to whether pastoral ministry, or something else should be his calling. As with the

Call to which I was commended, perhaps this was a negative for Tim too, that resulted in a positive outcome.

Son Tim decided to become an architect rather than a pastor. Thanks to a caring teacher at Woodbury Central High School, in Moville, Tim was allowed to advance his skills in computer science. Once Tim arrived at the School of Architecture at Ames, Iowa, he was given a grant to help implement an increase in computer literacy.

After Tim became an architect, he was awarded a prize for creativity for the First Building Project he supervised. That seemed affirmation that he found the vocation in which he seems to find rich fulfillment. Knowing he's a PK, short for pastor's kid, he was often the lead in design and planning church buildings. Today he runs his own firm in Polk City, Iowa.

Justice, truth and faithfulness, signs and qualities of Christian ministry, may be interpreted differently depending on one's station in life and one's relationship to a particular issue. In this Jewell parish setting, one could peer out the window of that pastor's office and see what was once a nursing care center, but now was home for persons with other special needs. When I heard that there was an effort to close that home due to the character of those residents, and, therefore, also possibly affecting property values; concern for justice and fairness crept into my mind. Bible reading and Christian education do things like that!

Prophetic ministry requires a commitment to justice and truth. Concerns surfaced in my mind concerning procedures I'd heard about in trying to close that care center. My conscience nagged at me saying, "Are you going to just sit by and let what appears to be an injustice happen, or will you try to assert some prophetic leadership." In an effort to support the administrator of that facility with whom I had become acquainted due to conducting a few worship services for the residents, I requested to see court documents and learned of some of the concerns raised, which implicated the administrator.

Therefore, I went to him with the concerns that I was hearing. Each one had a logical explanation that could be interpreted in different ways. I will mention just a couple that got me in trouble for questioning those "legal proceedings." (Those prophetic messages of Scripture reinforced by seminary education were compelling me to try to be faithful and prophetic in terms of justice in that present situation). So, I asked the administrator, "What's your version of the story that you were beating a resident on the ground in the parking lot?" He responded, "That was probably the day that that resident was having a seizure, and I was holding his hands down so he wouldn't harm himself." It doesn't take much imagination to see how that action could be interpreted in different ways.

Another accusation was that he put a hammer lock on a resident at a local store to drag him out of the store. The administrator responded, "By phone I was told a resident was causing a disturbance, so I went there and no one would assist me so I did that."

In the book of Joshua, there's a touching story of misinterpretation. It's about the people on the east side of the Jordan River having built an altar. That disturbed the tribes settling in the Promised Land. Thinking that this small group on the other side was not being loyal to the God of Israel who had led them to this juncture after the forty years of wilderness travel—so distressed were those settled people that they raised a threat of war. Thankfully, before attacking that minority on the other side of the Jordan River, they sent Phineas, the priest, with ten others to discuss the issue. Turns out the altar issue had an entirely different meaning than that which almost precipitated war (Joshua 22:10ff). Discussion clarified that issue and prevented further discord.

In conclusion of the congregational meeting mentioned earlier, the vote went against me. Technically, as I recall, it was not by a majority strong enough to dismiss me;

but the better part of wisdom it seemed was to resign. The Bishop, present for the meeting, apologized for not speaking to the congregation prior to the vote. It could be the Bishop thought there were more people there to support me than there were who opposed me. What he may not have realized is that there were several people there who otherwise were not usual attenders at worship. They had been urged by a community leader to be there for the vote.

After the vote, the Bishop and I had a brief discussion in the pastor's office. He suggested that I go to a counseling center for evaluation. (His reasons were probably in my best interests in terms of helping commend me to another Call.) But his comment so disturbed me that I said, "Bishop, I'm going to try and forget that you ever said that." The point being, I knew what I'd done on the several issues, (others are not mentioned here) and truly believed I was exercising a prophetic ministry. In great respect for Bishops and their many responsibilities, that was one of a few times I respectfully protested a Bishop's counsel.

One issue in that congregation, which I hope has been corrected, is that the ushers finished seating people before the service and then went down to the basement to drink coffee. That seemed to me a negative behavior for children, youth and everyone else to observe in those ushers. When I challenged that practice, I was told that I should be grateful that the ushers stayed in the building because they used to be able to go up town for coffee during the early part of the service including the sermon and get back in time for the offering. (In another paragraph there's a beautiful sequel to this story.)

One mistake of which I'm readily aware, and feel a need to confess, is that there had been a funeral. One family didn't arrive until the casket was being removed from the worship center after the service. The casket was then opened in the narthex so the late arrivals could view the body. A seminary discussion came to mind that that practice of opening the casket after the service can open the grieving wounds the worship service was intended to help heal.

When I challenged that event, I was told, "We are big folks now, we can handle things like that." If I was to do that over, I would not have made any comment about that incident.

With a mysterious longing for understanding with those who opposed me and with gratitude toward those who seemed to view with compassion my pastoral work, I remember those days with mixed emotions.

Abe, one of the ushers stood up among his peers at a previous congregational meeting in the church basement. That meeting had probably been called to sort out some of the issues before that afore mentioned meeting to vote on my tenure in that congregation. Abe said, "Come on fellows, we go down and drink coffee during the worship service after getting the people ushered into worship and then we go through the line after worship and compliment the pastor on his sermon. Come on fellows, we didn't listen to the sermon. We were down there talking about the weather, sports and such things."

That bold confession in front of a basement full of his church associates stands out as something so beautiful that it made that two-year ministry worthwhile. Abe's confession was not only honest and courageous, but also vindication of something I had challenged and was rebuffed.

Wow! Thanks, Abe, for that bold confession. Abe has since gone to his eternal home.

CHAPTER NINE
A Teacher's Delight

*"Therefore go and make disciples of all nations, ... and teaching
them to obey everything I have commanded you"*
(Matthew 28:20).

Teaching has always been a highlight of pastoral ministry for me. You may recall from a precious chapter that at the Christian Business Men's Center in Oceanside, California, I attended a Bible Study in which I felt a mysterious sense of being anointed for teaching the Bible; but, as I said in that chapter, I had no idea how that would unfold into the future. This Call seemed to be a part of the revealing and unfolding.

In this next new setting, I was at least the second person interviewed as they were selecting their next pastor to Call. What a joy it was that I could be affirmed for such a Call after having the last Call terminated by a congregational vote. I've chosen to believe that the Bishop affirmed my fitness as a pastor in spite of the dismissal in my last Call. Thank you, Bishop! Joys continue to multiply as a result of those ten plus years at that parish in Parkersburg.

Expectations of a new pastor in this Call to Bethel Lutheran of Parkersburg exceeded my expectations in terms of what I would have dared to propose as a teaching ministry involving youth. This happened to be a moment in time when the ELCA (Evangelical Lutheran Church in America) confession of the Christian faith was promoting longer and later confirmation. At this moment of writing, I re-experience the soaring feelings I had that I could be part of such a ministry. Some very thoughtful young parents in this congregation saw the opportunity for their children in longer and later confirmation, and they developed the program they wanted for their children; and I became the fortunate pastor to help them put that into practice.

They wanted confirmation classes to begin in the fifth grade for their children and continue through the ninth grade. In the fifth and sixth grade, the expectation would be for parents to be present for six weeks of class in the fall and again in the spring. Parental presence would be optional for grades seven through nine. Oh, what a challenge and joy to meet with parents and their children to discuss the essentials of a saving faith in Jesus who wants to be their personal savior and Lord.

When Called, after that interview, we moved from Jewell, Iowa, to Parkersburg, Iowa. Precious memories linger from meeting and working with many loving and dedicated people in Jewell; in spite of the termination process. Several years later, four members of that Jewell parish drove approximately 100 miles to help me celebrate the fortieth anniversary of my Ordination. One couple came at least twice from Jewell to Parkersburg, previous to the 40th anniversary celebration, to make sure we were surviving and thriving well after that short-term experience in their parish setting.

The longer and later confirmation program at Bethel Lutheran of Parkersburg was a great experience in youth ministry for me. In addition, the congregation had an after-school program for children to spend an hour at church once a week. We called it BLAST: Bethel Lutheran After School Teaching. Such positive programing does not happen without congregational support and the involvement of faithful and caring people.

Through the years, I've witnessed blessed partnerships between individuals in congregations, partners who have won the support of the congregational leadership and do so many wonderful things together. Two individuals in that congregation stand out in my mind. They were a blessed partnership for accomplishing beautiful spiritually enriching goals for that Bethel Lutheran congregation. One night they were working so late on a project in the Worship Center that I felt guilty going home while they, the unpaid volunteers, were laboring together at that hour. To assuage my guilt, I went home and with my wife's counsel arranged to take them a sweet treat for their efforts. They expressed appreciation for that gesture of gratitude.

We did lose two families to another congregation because they did not accept the Longer and Later Confirmation Program for their children. One Board member suggested that I go to their home to discuss their dissatisfaction. They had made up their mind, so it seems my visit to them was not helpful. Thankfully, the church board and congregation did not allow the loss of two families to derail that otherwise positive program.

The timing of coming to Bethel Lutheran of Parkersburg seemed perfect. Although one day, I remember parking my car in the garage and saying to myself, "I think I have jumped from the frying pan into the fire." Seems I've often been placed in situations where there's a need for reconciliation ministry. In the holy Christian church: "We are entrusted with the ministry of reconciliation" (2 Corinthians 5:17ff).

Recently, I read the story of Thomas Aquinas (1224/25-1274) who at age 19 wanted to join the Dominican order. This decision did not please his family. "Thomas was kidnapped by his brothers and held hostage by his family for almost two years. At one point, his family even attempted to seduce him with a prostitute they had hired for the purpose! Eventually, however, his mother gave in and helped him escape out a window one evening. Thomas quickly made his way back to Naples and from there went to Rome. Finally, in 1245, he ended up in Paris, where the chair of the theology department was Albertus Magnus, who was also a Dominican" (Professor Dorsey Armstrong, Ph.D. *Great Minds of the Medieval World*, 2014, P. 297). Imagine the need for reconciliation in just that one situation.

A Robin Messenger

A construction project was initiated in this parish to add handicap access to the building. That was a time of great joy to witness congregational members working together on that project.

One Sunday morning, however, while contemplating one of the administrative issues creating some tension, I had walked to the main entrance to look down the sidewalk by which people would soon be coming to worship. At the moment, I was preoccupied with a complex issue that had dragged me into some despondency. Troubling thoughts had surfaced in my mind about my future in that congregational setting. I believe the Holy Spirit motivated me to take a walk to the main entrance that morning.

At the very moment, while contemplating the troubling dilemma, a large plump robin appeared on the porch step within three feet of where I was standing. It seemed he wanted to enter the church building. At its appearance, a perfect peace settled over me as though an angel had caressed my soul. That robin I interpreted as a divine messenger.

That robin's appearance was momentous for that particular morning's distress. Additionally, however, ever since that moment, robins seemed to have appeared whenever I've needed extra encouragement and reassurance. That has happened so many times and in so many settings—too numerous to mention. In the summer, as I drive out of the alley on my way to work now in Waterloo, Iowa, so often there's a robin or two along the way; sometimes a flock. For several weeks I've been wanting to see a robin perfectly poised for a good picture. My wife and I have had a rental property for sale and have been mildly distressed that no one seemed interested. One evening a robin appeared along the street a couple of blocks from that property. After stopping by the curb, getting out and positioning my cell phone for a picture, the robin flew away. So I walked down the street past the rental property and a whole flock of robins flew off the yard. The next day we got our first offer on the property which resulted in the sale.

At this time, I do have a picture of a robin on my iPhone. It was another moment of contemplation, in another city, relating to a personal financial risk decision. A relatively large bird was perched on a rock looking in the opposite direction so I could not see the breast. But something hinted in my mind to walk around to check the front of the bird—seemingly too large to be a robin. But the bird stayed put until I could get a good look—it was a robin! So, I snapped the picture. That red-breasted bird was as plump as the robin at the entry of the church building a few years ago.

It seemed another of those moments when the Lord of Life had sent a messenger at just the right moment for my need of reassurance. He gives that extra assurance by various means, I believe, to every one of his faithful disciples according to their particular needs and circumstances.

Thank you, Lord, for a very special individual evening where the church basement was filled with people. A congregational meeting had been called to resolve a brewing conflict. As I sat beside the Bishop, he asked, "Whose side are all these people on?" All I could say was, "I'm not really sure." The meeting began. At the meeting a son of an early spokesman at the meeting said, "That's enough, Dad." His dad was castigating me for something. Once that son cooled his dad's passion, another man stood up and spoke eloquently like I'd never heard him speak before. After his speech, the meeting soon adjourned and life moved on. Both sides had had their opportunity to express themselves—in my view it was all a spinoff of that bold initiative to implement that Longer and Later Confirmation Program.

We had recently had a meeting of the concerned persons regarding Longer and Later Confirmation. It probably should not be surprising that with such a major shift in youth programming, that there might be some reactions. I had proposed three options to resolve the issues I'd overheard being discussed: 1) forget the new program and have the committee start from scratch to propose a new program. Prior to my arrival a committee had been formed because some members wanted a stronger program, or 2) press on with what we have as it is; or 3) press on with what we have as it is and make whatever adjustments that seem to be needed as suggested by those involved along the way into the future.

One parent stood up during that meeting and said, "My only objection to the program is that I don't want to be attending seventh grade confirmation with my daughter." Since that was not a requirement, only an option, it turned out to be a non-issue. The meeting dismissed.

My Wife Remembers

My dear wife remembers the day at meal time (after worship) when I was being chastised during a phone conversation. The phone had rung during our Sunday meal time. Ella, my dear wife, remembers that our daughter who happened to be home from college at that time overheard words spoken by the caller. The hurtful part was seeing our daughter's tears because she was pained by the way that man was talking to her father. Evidently she could hear the loud voice of the man on the other end of that call. Pastors sometimes need to stand firm with a kind and gracious spirit toward those who would end the democratic process and try to manipulate the pastor to their point of view. Seemingly that was the intent of the voice on the phone that Sunday.

Thanks be to our risen Lord for a mother in that parish who on another occasion went to the office of the Bishop and spoke on my behalf when I wouldn't let myself be manipulated by a pressure group to do their bidding. That mother represented the younger families who wanted the new program for their children. Interestingly, in the former parish some of the more articulate assertive leaders were opposing me; in this parish several of the more articulate, assertive leaders were supporting their pastor.

Pressure groups can give the impression they speak for the official board and for the majority, but that may be far from the truth. A visitor to my office one day accused me of not listening, but my interpretation of that conversation is that the decision was made by using the democratic process in regard to the Longer and Later Confirmation Program and that man tried his best to modify the decision.

At the time, I had some empathy with the man putting pressure on me. He was a loyal church member and a grandfather. Because his son and family left the congregation due to not accepting the Longer and Later Confirmation Program; however, I could not let my empathy with that man (knowing that he wouldn't be sitting with his son and grandchildren in the near future at worship) derail the democratic process by which that program became reality. Such are among the occasional complexities of pastoral leadership.

A surprise challenge presented itself when it came time to follow through once those precious youth had finished the Longer and Later Confirmation Program. No one seemed available to accept the role of teaching a high school Sunday School class. A few people taking turns for only a Sunday or two, seemed inconsistent with the commitment we had asked of our youth and their parents.

The only solution I could come up with, was to ask my dear wife to take on that challenge. She did that beautifully for the remainder of our years at that Call. We continued to hear stories of the positive impact she made as a Sunday School teacher. Sometimes there were as many as twenty plus students.

One room in the basement of that building became walls for the Christian message—Bible story pictures painted by those youth. We could walk through the room and remember who of that youth group painted that picture, and that picture and another. Their teacher's art major had expressed itself through her leadership in that situation.

Parking Lot/Coffee Klatch Conversations

"Put me on the council and I'll set that pastor straight," one man supposedly had said one morning over coffee. He got elected to the Board, but "Blessed Be the Tie that Binds." Once again, one woman with strong Christian values spoke boldly to him at a board meeting and life moved on. Though a community leader, not a regular church attendee, he couldn't dominate that Board of committed church leaders. What a joy it is to know that one is surrounded and supported by persons who know the purpose of the church, it's administrative and constitutional mandates, affirms it values, and asserts leadership consistent with those guidelines. One man with another agenda could not derail those intentions put in place by the democratic process.

Soon there was an unfortunate death a mile or so from town and as pastor I was called to the farm. That man who would "set me straight," now called the employees together there in the barn, and we joined hands in prayer around the tragedy that had occurred earlier that day. What a blessing to witness a man, once seemingly my nemesis, with the character and courage to rally the employees together for prayer there in the barn. I had never had a prayer meeting in a barn before or since.

Another man, with his family, had transferred into the congregation from a Waterloo congregation and began to try to tailor Bethel Lutheran committee meetings after that larger city congregation he had transferred from in Waterloo. So determined was he, that eventually, even as the folks seemed content with the committee meeting schedules as they were, this man seemed to have concluded that the pastor had an unnecessary control over those groups. In his mind that was the reason they wouldn't budge from their convictions. His conclusion of excessive pastoral control seemed related to the reality that he could not persuade the groups to change their committee meeting time. That, in my opinion, was his inaccurate interpretation (that the pastor had inordinate control). The people were simply content with the present committee structure. Consequently, pushing his perception of the issue to the limit, he persuaded the board to request that I, the pastor, not attend committee meetings. So, with that message conveyed to me by the board at an officially called meeting, also termed council, I left that meeting and returned within a few minutes with a letter of resignation indicating that if I could not be pastor to the people at committee meetings, I could no longer serve the congregation as their pastor. I left the letter with them and returned to the parsonage just a few feet away from the entrance to the church building. As I had just arrived home, the doorbell rang, and the president, bless her, said, "This is not what we want. Please withdraw this letter." So, I did. And once again, life moved on.

Incidentally, my mother had died while we were serving that congregation in Parkersburg. She lived in Osseo, Wisconsin, approximately two-hundred miles from Parkersburg. Ella and I had travelled there for the funeral celebrating the life of my godly and talented mother. While exiting the family prayer room, prior to the worship service, and while entering the worship center, I caught a glimpse of the woman, the president of the congregation back in Parkersburg, who had driven that distance to show respect to her pastor and his mother at this time of grieving. Tears welled in my eyes as I experienced that moment of compassion.

During our pastorate at Bethel Lutheran, the congregation gave their approval for me to pursue a Doctor of Ministry degree. That involved trips to Omaha for classes and eventually thirty days on the Drew University Campus in

New Jersey. (One day a family member was showing me pictures they had taken of me during that graduation ceremony.) "Where am I in the picture?" I asked. "Right there," they said, pointing to the man facing the front; but he had a head of gray hair. That was a new perspective since I hadn't seen a picture of me from the back before and didn't realize how gray headed I had become. Along with emotional peaks and valleys, there were evidently chemical changes, too, in this earthly temple (St. Paul's term) that we call our body.

My doctrinal thesis was on the theme "Justified and Working for Justice." Lutherans are very much focused on justification by grace through faith (Romans 5 and Ephesians 2:8ff). The motive for my thesis was (and is) that justification by faith needs to result in boldness and Christian caring and working for justice.

Also during those years, the congregation responded positively to a news item from the Lutheran Immigration and Refugee Service—probably passed on to us from the Synod office. The congregation then sponsored a family from Romania who were religiously persecuted, the Sava family. To this day, twenty-five years later, they continue to keep in touch. If you ever do business at CVS Pharmacy, you may have purchased items handled by the Sava daughters who work for that company in Knoxville, Tennessee, (at least they did for some time).

We were called to attend the funeral of the head of that family, Mr. Sava, a very devout Pentecostal man with a similarly devout family. Only after we arrived did I realize they wanted me to bring a message at that service. We have received several gifts from them and have at times reminded the congregation, Bethel Lutheran of Parkersburg, of the gratitude that family continues to express for the church's sponsorship that allowed them to come to America.

One man, Laurentu, was also with the group. He was an agricultural worker and manager of a commune in Romania. He was quite an eccentric man; and while we are quite certain he has remained in Iowa, neither he nor we have kept in touch. His abilities shown through, however, as he nurtured the finest garden we had ever seen in the small patch of ground between the church building and the parsonage. He'd even get up during the night (he stayed with us in the parsonage for a while) to water the garden when needed.

During our years at Parkersburg, a member of that congregation had fulfilled her term on the Lutheran Student Center board, Cedar Falls, Iowa—home of UNI (University of Northern Iowa). She asked if I would like to be her replacement, which I felt greatly honored to do. Six years on that board, three as chair, gave me some experience with that ministry. That connection continues to enrich my life through memories, reports, and occasional contacts with others who served at that time and continue to serve that ministry to UNI students. As of this writing, I now have the privilege of serving as chaplain at a long-term care center, two blocks down the street from that student center, and I often pass by that campus center while carrying out pastoral duties.

Folks who know the area of Parkersburg, also know of two tragedies which struck that community within the next few years. One was a tornado which leveled much of the town. The rebuilding process was so spectacular that the part of the town most devastated by the tornado now looks like a brand-new development.

Several of the church buildings in that town were built on a line east to west, perhaps not intentionally, but the tornado leveled much of the town to the south of that line with comparatively little damage to the church buildings and the buildings north of that line.

A second event making headlines in Parkersburg within the last several years was the killing of Coach Thomas. Coach Thomas, though a small-town football coach, he had several of his former players go on to the NFL. His Christian convictions and testimony were clear to those who knew him well. We invited him and he spoke at one of our Bethel Lutheran Youth group meetings.

Tragically, a former player, yet high school age, walked into the makeshift workout area (makeshift due to the tornado devastation) and shot Coach Thomas while he was supervising and working out with his players. There's now a new law on the books passed by the state legislature, initiated by the Coach Thomas family, that relates to more observation of certain troubled folks being released from mental health centers. That coach's story is further elucidated in a book titled, *The Sacred Acre*.

CHAPTER TEN
Rich Rewards in Perseverance

"Do not lag in zeal, be ardent in spirit, serve the Lord"
(Romans 12:11).

After ten plus years and many other blessed experiences at Bethel Lutheran of Parkersburg, it seemed a good time to resign. At the time, I was sixty-three years old; and we had purchased a house in Waterloo. A brief time in Waterloo without a full-time job/call commitent told me that retirement was not for me. Therefore, I was exceedingly grateful for the opportunity to serve half time as youth coordinator and visitation pastor at Trinity Lutheran in Waterloo. Thanks to that pastor who trusted me to be an associate in that ministry. That half-time position also allowed some time to do pulpit supply and interim ministry. Eventually that included an interim ministry at the Lutheran Student Center in Cedar Falls (where I had previously served on the board for six years), while they processed a Call to someone to fill the vacancy left by the beloved Campus Pastor John Deines.

Trinity Lutheran had an after-school program bringing in dozens of children from the community. That congregation also has a gym as part of the building facility, which lends itself well to such an after-school program. Thankfully, the congregation also had a follow-through program for youth after confirmation. Two compassionate women guided that program.

Ella and I joined the choir very soon after joining the congregation. One member of the congregation had a vineyard in Germany, and he had fallen in love with the housekeeper of that castle on the vineyard. He greatly appreciated the Trinity Lutheran choir and wanted them to sing at his wedding in Germany so he made arrangements to fly us there. However, that woman decided she didn't want to live in America, so the wedding was cancelled. Nevertheless, this man followed through on his original plan to finance the trip to Germany for the whole choir and to see other sights and countries; and then the return trip to Waterloo. We felt blessed to be a part of that trip.

On a less joyful note, one day as I arrived to give private communion to a resident in a local care facility, I entered the resident's room to discover her face appeared totally black and blue. So vivid were those colors of her face they have left a lasting impression in my mind and a motive for counsel to some elderly people. "What happened?" I asked. "Well," she said, "I was trying to put my slacks on without sitting down or leaning on anything." She got off balance and down she went evidently slamming her face on the floor. That drama has been a personal lesson for me and one I've passed on to others as I've had opportunity while working with many senior citizens: take time to sit while dressing with slacks, socks, and such pull-ons.

Home communions, often an associate pastor's assigned duty, provide many opportunities for conversation on very personal matters and community concerns.

One dear lady had a picture of her husband on the wall, but would never speak of him. One day when I arrived for one of her in-home communion visits, she was emotionally distraught.

The building of the Isle of Capri Casino on the southeast edge of Waterloo was in the news and hearing that news opened a whole pent up bag of memory issues for this woman. She said she had known that her husband did some gambling before they moved to Waterloo from Kansas City, but had no idea the extent of his gambling involvement. One day he was invited to another state to meet with persons to whom he evidently owed gambling debts. The story was that he was expected to sign over his business enterprise in that city where they had lived prior to her settling in Waterloo. Since he refused to sign over his business, he was later found beheaded in his car near that city to which he had been invited to consult about those gambling debts.

Now this woman, living in an apartment by herself was reliving the grief and shock of those former days. That's the story this woman (now deceased) conveyed to me that day.

That story is one more memory that has made me an anti-gambling, anti-Casino person. Thankfully, most denominations have strong anti-gambling social statements that help call attention to the negative side of the gambling industry.

While enjoying the pastoral work with the blessed folks of Trinity Lutheran in the year 2000, another opportunity opened up for me. There was a need for someone to do supply chaplaincy at the Cedar Falls Lutheran Home. That chaplain, Pastor David, was retiring and needed someone to supply while he took some accumulated vacation time. It has always been a mystery, to me, as to why I was contacted for that need since to my knowledge I had never met Pastor David, the soon-to-retire chaplain.

Chaplaincy had always been at the bottom of my list of ways to serve as an ordained person. However, after two weeks of supply ministry at the Care Center, a few residents suggested to the administration that I might be an appropriate successor to their chaplain who was planning to retire soon. Long story short, that was sixteen years ago, and I've been richly blessed to serve at that facility.

Within the last few years, that care center has been re-named NewAldaya Lifescapes. Cedar Falls Lutheran

Home was the original name. For marketing purposes the name was changed. With the new name persons interested in residing there would not feel the facility was only for Lutherans, or only for Cedar Falls residents.

What a privilege it continues to be to serve in an enterprise within our culture as it is today and to serve with a mission statement that reads, "Christian Caring: enhancing lives through a commitment to individualized care in a home empowered by God's love." In our world today, where some are not permitted to express their faith on the job, or wear a cross, plus so many other media enticements that contradict the morality of Christian faith, it is a joy to see such a mission statement even on the vehicles used to transport residents, and to know that all employees are expected to fulfill that quality of caring.

Now I needed to resign my Call to serve at Trinity Lutheran of Waterloo, also having served there briefly as interim, while a new Call was extended to replace their pastor who recently retired. "The wind blows where it chooses..." (John 3:8).

NewAldaya Lifescapes has a strategic—minded executive director who maintains and implements programs, with board support, to make such a place, a place to "Live Better and Live Well." She has recently received the highest Leading Age honor award they ever give to anyone.

After ten years of chaplaincy and in my mid-seventies, it seemed to me that someone else should have the opportunity to serve that chaplaincy Call. In a letter to the Bishop, I indicated my intention to resign from the chaplaincy at the end of 2010, but would like the opportunity to serve in a parish setting. (Discontinuing full-time ministry, while my health continued to be strong didn't seem appropriate to me.) Consequently, my name was submitted to First Lutheran of Waterloo, a once large congregation with a beautiful facility; but now an elderly community with an average age of around eighty years. (Incidentally, a former pastor there had also been the most recent long-term chaplain at the Cedar Falls Lutheran Home.)

Community changes such as plant closings and an increasingly multi-ethnic population, and the four lane, Martin Luther King Jr. Highway, within a few yards from the building (that several of the congregation say took away the neighborhood feeling) all took its toll on the membership of the congregation. Recently I was riding with a man who pointed to a sports field area near the church building and he said, "I remember when the area was filled with houses."

A unique feature of that lovely building is a large mosaic of Jesus (probably thirty plus feet in height) with outstretched arms facing east as though inviting every passerby along Martin Luther King Jr. Highway and High Street to come "unto him." David Delafield is credited with developing that beautiful piece of art. On the Internet site one finds these words, "His works of art may be found throughout the Waterloo/Cedar Falls communities."

For a few years, the congregation had only short term pastorates, and most recently, Sunday by Sunday fill ins. Knowing that was not a healthy situation and with there being a shortage of pastors, I committed for at least five years—if they wanted me to serve them that long. Counsel through the Synod staff was that this should be a Call renewable year by year in the event they or I would want out of the Call. Each year they have unanimously renewed the Call for me to continue there. Now that the five years of pastoral service has been fulfilled, they have been assured that as long as they approve, I'll continue with them as long as I'm at NewAldaya as chaplain.

Once that Call to First Lutheran was extended and accepted ("The wind blows where it chooses..." John 3:8), I felt totally convinced that I should continue as chaplain at NewAldaya Lifescapes with that regular schedule of Tuesday, Thursday, and Friday morning Chapel Services; Wednesday afternoon Vespers, plus Sunday morning 10:30

worship in their beautiful Chapel; and Sunday late afternoon Worship Services in two memory care secured units:
along with other pastoral care responsibilities for staff and
residents. Ella and I worship at 8:30 a.m. at First Lutheran,
so we travel to NewAldaya in Cedar Falls (approximately
seven miles) after worship and a brief time of fellowship in
the Chapel. That fellowship includes Bible Study twice a
month.

While it sounds presumptuous that I should be so
honored, I do believe the Holy Spirit set me aside long
enough to commit to First Lutheran and their special need
for consistent pastoral care.

Signs we interpret as blessings of the Holy Spirit
upon the First Lutheran congregation include: the Prairie
Lakes Multi-Site Ministry Group (previously the Baptist
congregation in downtown Cedar Falls), which asked and
was granted the opportunity to rent the First Lutheran facility. They worship at 11 a.m. bringing in two hundred plus
folks including many children and youth. They have also
spent much money enhancing the interior of the First Lutheran facility, especially the basement area which had been
neglected due to First Lutheran no longer having a viable
Sunday School and youth ministry. Prairie Lakes Ministry
has also installed air conditioning in the First Lutheran
building. The First Lutheran board reminds them, and the
board members themselves, that these are investments
Prairie Lakes has chosen for their ministry and were approved, though not requested by First Lutheran.

(Unexpectedly, as of this moment of editing, the an-
nouncement has been made that Prairie Lakes is leaving
First Lutheran and has just announced for their congregation to join Hope City Church along University Avenue,
which congregation has outgrown their facility and may
want to rent and possibly buy the First Lutheran building.)

Further, we interpret as a timely blessing, an awesome soloist who intones the Psalms at least once each
month. First Lutheran also has attracted the commitment of

Butch (we call him our own Pavarotti) who brings a powerful message in song every third Sunday.

These are among the obvious visible blessings we like to claim as encouragement to remain steadfast in ministry in that multi-ethnic community, across the parking lot from one of the two public high schools in the Waterloo area. Also, recently due to relatively minor hail damage to the roof over the newest part of the facility, the insurance paid for an entire new roof.

First Lutheran also has a very energetic president who has been bringing her elderly mother to worship. Once her mother is seated, this lady takes charge of Altar Guild responsibilities; with some assistance from one or two others. (As of the last few months, this elderly mother has not been able for health reasons to attend morning worship; and we have recently hosted the funeral for this dear elderly and faithful member of the congregation.) That president's encouragement and lively leadership helps encourage the congregation along with a faithful usher group and drivers who bring a few persons who need transportation; and not to neglect mentioning a faithful spiritually concerned six-member board.

A recent blessing in the chaplaincy ministry at NewAldaya has been to have twenty residents sign on and have now completed the two-year Bethel Bible Series program. Three of the twenty had died during that time. What a joy and delight to see so many in the seventh and eighth decades of their life (one soon to be one hundred years old) continue to be hungering and thirsting for more of God's grace through the precious miracle of our Lord's written Word.

Yes, the miracle of the written word! In her book, *Great Minds of the Medieval World*, Professor Dorsey Armstrong reminds her readers, "What we have to remember here is that at this time, all books were painstakingly made by hand: an animal had to be slaughtered, skinned, its hide stretched and scraped, smoothed with a pumice stone, cut into sheets, and then the words carefully written in beautiful but painstaking form." On the next page, she states that it took 2000 cattle to produce enough pages to make a beautiful Bible. "The reason we know this is because in that year Wearmouth-Jarrow sought and procured a land grant with the specific purpose of raising 2,000 head of cattle on it. Why did he need 2,000 cattle? Well the answer is, that was how many you needed to produce enough vellum pages to make a beautiful Bible. Seventh-century book production is a long way, indeed, from the modern printing press and downloadable texts." (pp. 84-85).

What a gift it is to have the Bible and its message to study and pass along, especially when remembering the labor-intensive process of ancient writing techniques.

Another joy of chaplaincy at NewAldaya is the ecumenicity of the community. A delightful Irish Catholic woman wanted her funeral at the NewAlaya Lifescapes Chapel. Her daughter from an eastern state helped to facilitate the funeral planning. She requested that my wife sing the Lord's Prayer at that Celebration of Life Service. The deacon who officiated the service invited all present, regardless of denomination, to receive the Sacrament as this dear humorous Irish Catholic always did each month in our NewAldaya Chapel. Pope Francis has recently completed his visit to the United States and has made many feel his presence as a healing force toward greater unity among all Christian denominations.

We practice ecumenicity consistently at NewAldaya Lifescapes. Besides the NewAldaya Ecumenical openness, sharing a Lutheran owned facility with the Baptist Prairie Lakes Ministries has been a challenge related to Christian unity within the body of Christ. Our goal with Prairie Lakes has been to focus upon the Great Commission rather than perspectives on Baptism or any other potentially divisive issues. Throughout the years of teaching youth in confirmation, I would remind them we all know wonderful Christian friends and neighbors who are of various denominations.

Quite obviously the Lord has blessed their life and ministry too. My father's youngest sister, Corrine, married a Catholic man in the 1950s. That caused a significant disruption in the family structure, at least at the conversation level. At this time, there is an orphanage in Africa with a plaque in memory of Corrine who helped to raise money in America to build the orphanage. Though baptized in the Lutheran confession of Christian faith and the only one of the large family to convert to Catholicism, she has left a stellar legacy.

Along with these rich ministry experiences, I'm also remembering my pastor back home when asked when he would retire, his response was "The Lord will decide." By that I believe he meant as long as health and circumstances allowed he'd keep on serving as pastor of those three rural and one small town congregation. In approximately the forty-fifth year of his ministry, he helped to organize a fourth congregation. This fourth congregation was in the small town of Hixton, Wisconsin. One of the members of that congregation became an assistant to the Bishop here in Iowa. Many probably remember the witty and pastoral Richard Thompson. He was one of the far-reaching rewards of the faithful ministry of Pastor E.B. Christopherson.

Also, at NewAldaya, a professor of education at UNI, helped initiate a program known as S.A.G.E. Those letters stand for Seniors Acquiring Intergenerational Experience. Seniors at UNI who plan to teach and who are interested in S.A.G.E. are assigned to a resident at NewAldaya, most of whom would be in their seventh, eighth, and several in their ninth decade of life. Questions are assigned for discussion for each of seven visits between the UNI senior and the resident. Sometime after the seventh sessions have been completed there is a S.A.G.E. graduation ceremony at NewAldaya at which each participant gets a copy of a book in which participants have recorded their interpretation of their experience. We learn much from the student's perspective;

and the students indicate that the visits have been enlightening for them.

Crumbs from the Master's Table

After the woman in Matthew 15:21-28 made her somewhat spunky response Jesus commended her, and her daughter was healed.

Presently at eighty plus years of age and serving a full-time and a part-time Call there's been such joy and fulfillment in pastoral ministry that discontinuing does not have much appeal.

A very positive force in continuing these several years beyond a frequent cut off of sixty plus years has been the very positive support of my faithful wife. She also seems to find fulfillment and joy in many interactions with the wonderful people with whom we serve. Many prayer requests are passed along for us to share and ask for healing in varied situations.

At least one Sunday evening a month after the fourth worship service of the day (8:30 a.m. First Lutheran; 10:30 a.m. at NewAldaya; and two late afternoon dementia/memory care services), Ella accompanies me to take home communion to five different home settings on behalf of First Lutheran congregation of Waterloo and occasionally accompanies me on other home communion visits. She also is the household manager, business manager of rental properties, and a great support person for the work I've felt called to do.

Her career path, after degrees from Morningside College in Sioux City in art and business, began with both part-time and then full-time employment in Sioux City. One of those full-time positions was managing a political campaign for the campaign candidate for whom she was office manager.

Once we moved to Jewell, Iowa, she became employed as a translator within the Sauer Sundstrand Company in Ames, Iowa. That company has an affiliate in Germany. Since Ella had a German language background (her first language as a child was German), and due to spending her first years in Europe before coming to America as part of a refugee family; she had the necessary skills for translation. (That background as part of a refugee family has incited some of her (our) passion to assist refugees.)

More Crumbs from the Master's Table

While Ella was commuting eighty plus miles one way to Ames from Parkersburg, it seemed prudent to purchase, at her suggestion, a property there that we could rent to Iowa State students and, in which, she could reserve a room for herself in case of inclement weather that would make travel an unnecessary risk. That was a relatively successful venture into rental property, which provided an incentive to pursue that more extensively which we have done thanks, in part, to her business and interior decorating interest and expertise. Her college major in business and art has helped to bring many rewards into our marriage and family life.

One day Ella was aboard an airplane and sitting beside a Korean lady with whom Ella shared the information that we had a rental property for sale in Ames. (Eighty miles was a pretty long commute now that we had moved to Parkersburg, and we thought it best to sell that Ames Queen Ann-style house), especially since Ella was downsized out of her position in the Ames firm. This lady aboard the plane beside Ella was enthusiastically interested in the Ames property because her husband had a Christian ministry both in Ames and in Waterloo where we were living at that time. Long story short, they purchased that property with the understanding that Ella would provide consulting advice to them for at least one year.

In the year 1991, we made a trip to Germany so that we, with Ella's mother, could visit relatives who chose to stay in East Germany. The Berlin Wall had come down and Check Point Charley at that time was growing up in weeds. There was then more freedom to travel between East and

West Germany. One cousin in East Germany had an immediate question for Ella, "Was your father the one who knocked on our window that night and asked whether we wanted to leave Germany with them?" That answer was "Yes, that was my father."

Since under communism many church buildings had been converted to other uses. The church building in Britzke, the home town of Ella's relatives, had been converted into a granary. Her relatives were eager to show us now that communism had failed in East Germany their progress in renovating their local church building. In the process, they discovered that previous custodians of that property had painted over beautiful art work. So, they discontinued their scraping and redecorating to hire a professional to evaluate and authenticate the date and quality of those paintings.

Due to an eighteenth century-long dry season in Germany, many Germans left that country and settled in Romania where Ella's parents were born as were her older siblings. That story reminds us of the ancient Israelites who left their homeland for similar reasons (Genesis 42-43) related to weather.

Stalin did not trust Hitler so he insisted that the Germans leave Romania so in the case of Ella's family, they fled to Poland where Ella and her two younger siblings were born. Once the news came that a Russian army would travel through that town in Poland to help defeat Hitler, the mayor of that town organized those people and led them into Germany. He probably could have fled to safety himself, but he cared for his people and wouldn't leave them behind to be overrun by the Russian army knowing how that might affect women, children and others. Thus, the next few years, the Rauter family remained in Germany for several years before coming to America under the auspices of Lutheran World Action.

One of the counter forces to the secular emphasis of communism which had disrupted so many families is YWAM (Youth With A Mission). YWAM is the largest para church ministry in existence. It was founded by Loren Cunningham and now operates in more than 650 centers in 135 countries. The story of the founding of YWAM is told in the book *Is That Really You God? by* Loren Cunningham (June, 2011).

Ella and I became aware of YWAM in a somewhat unusual way. We had just moved into Waterloo, on Third Street, a home we thought might be our home for the remainder of our lives. "The best laid plans of men and mice sometimes go astray" (Robert Burns). One day we noticed that the large two and one half story house across the alley had gone on the market. Just out of curiosity we asked for a tour. Once inside the house built in 1919, we discovered beautiful woodwork and a fire place. We immediately thought this would make a great mission house. We really wanted to live there. So, we made the necessary financial arrangements to make that move.

One day there was a knock on the door. A YWAM couple asked to see the upstairs because they had read on the Internet that we were a Living Waters Retreat site of the Northeast Iowa Synod of the ELCA (Evangelical Church of America). In other words, we would host without cost to pastors in distress and/or missionaries on leave. Since I answered the door that day and Ella was across the alley, I said, "Ella is showing a house we have for sale, but you can go upstairs here and check it out for your needs." Their immediate response was, "Do you have a house for sale? We are looking for a house to buy." They bought that house Ella was showing to prospective buyers across the alley. This YWAM couple are now our neighbors. As YWAM missionaries they have completed a tour in France; and most recently in Mongolia.

We had never heard of YWAM. So, over an evening meal we asked about YWAM. The International Training Center is, they said, at Kona, Hawaii. "Really! We are scheduled to vacation at Kona, Hawaii, within the year."

One day, several years ago, I had asked Ella, "Is there anywhere you want to travel that you have not been." She indicated that she'd like to see Hawaii. So, for several years we have vacationed in Hawaii. Since becoming aware of YWAM we also visit the University of the Nations—the YWAM training center. Around a memorial pole at the University of the Nations, one can see a memorial stone we gave in honor of Byron and Sondra Simar, our first YWAM missionary friends.

One day one of their two children was standing with his father Byron in our driveway and Byron asked his son, "Are you ready for another relationship now after your divorce, I need to know how to pray for you?" His son said, "Yes." Ella overheard that response and introduced that son to her niece. They are now happily married and living in the state of Michigan.

"*Daring to Live on the Edge: The Adventure of Faith and Finance*" by Loren Cunningham (YWAM Founder), tells how his thousands of mission warriors serve without salary. He also tells of some of the creative circumstances in which those funds become available as they learn to trust Almighty God for their needs.

A portion of this writing is happening while we are at Cancun, Mexico, a favorite vacation site once we realized that the climate is about the same as Hawaii; and the time and expense of travel is quite a bit less.

When folks become aware of our January vacation habit to this ideal place, Cancun, Mexico, at the beautiful Grand Mayan Resort in the midst of the jungle, I like to remind them that working full time plus up to, and beyond eighty years of age, does provide some extra funds for such a vacation; along with the tithe and offerings for good causes such as YWAM. St. Paul's words remind that audience, and us, to work in order to help those in need.

There's a saying nowadays, that eighty is the new sixty. The suggested implication is that when people care well for their health, many can do at eighty what they previously could not do beyond at sixty. Many modern innovations and conveniences help us so barring accident, disease, or body abuse due to certain employment demands, or careless habits, many can do at age eighty years of age, what people struggled to do at sixty decades ago.

One of my passions is to do research on health analytics. As a chaplain in a long-term care center, I work among health care givers and have the opportunity to conduct a staff devotion in which I try to connect biblical principles with commitment to quality care giving. In winding down this book, here are a couple of quotes from two such books. "New science and care protocols emerge daily, leading to more complexity than most practitioners can comprehend. Every dramatic new development, from personalized genetic medicine to robotics and telemedicine, opens up new frontiers, but confuse patients and their care givers." *Health Analytics: Gaining the Insights to Transform Health Care* by Jason Burke, Wiley (Location 283, Kindle Reader).

In chapter five, "Grasping the Brass Ring to Improve Healthcare through Analytics: the Fundamentals" Dwight McNeill writes, "The United States healthcare industry faces enormous challenges. Its outcomes are the worst of its peers in wealthy countries, its efficiency is the worst of any industry, and its customer engagement ratings are the worst of any industry. Although the industry is profitable overall, ranking fourteenth among the top 35 industries, it has difficulty converting these challenges into business opportunities to do good by improving the health of its customers while doing well for its stockholders" (*Analytics in Healthcare and the Lifesciences: Strategies,* ed. by Dwight McNeil, 2013, Location 915, Kindle Reader).

While I, and probably many others want to think of America as number one, such statements indicate several countries do a better job applying available knowledge to actual hands on patient care than does America.

On our spiritual journey, we face a similar challenge. Resources are readily available. Power for the pursuit of justice and mercy for all is available to every believer in Jesus Christ as Savior and Lord. Bold leadership calls for applying the Holy Spirit Power to everyday needs around the world.

A few examples have been set before us in this book. Thanks be to the Lord God for all the bold leadership of Christians before us through the centuries who have passed on the historic saving faith of Christ the Lord. That legacy has provided rich rewards of grace for all to receive and enjoy!

"ALL THINGS Through Christ"
(Philippians 4:13)

ACKNOWLEDGEMENTS

First and foremost, a special thanks to my wife for all her assistance. She has a keen memory and has helped to recall many specifics of times and places mentioned. Secondly, thanks to our three children John (school teacher); Timothy (architect); and Gretchen (public administration degree utilized in several creative endeavors) whose lives of engagement and faith (also eight grandchildren) have continued to bless us, their parents. Special thanks to Sue Schuerman for editing the book and for her helpful comments and written suggestions to improve the manuscript.

Finally, thanks to all the folks throughout the years who have nurtured, guided and challenged me to put into practice the art of being their pastor. Each step along the way has enlarged the reservoir of experience that in turn has helped to develop insights, experience, and knowledge for the next step of the journey.

A major jumping off point in motivation to put some of my spiritual journey in this book came early in my ministry from the book *Pastor to Pastor* written by a former Rocky Mountain Synod bishop of the Lutheran Confession of the Christian faith. His down-to-earth practical thoughts helped to jumpstart my confidence in doing pastoral work; and created in me a hope to someday offer encouragement to others who may have a similar need.